ODD

by Hal Corley

A Samuel French Acting Edition

Founded 1830

New York Hollywood London Toronto

SAMUELFRENCH.COM

Copyright © 2007, 2009 by Hal Corley

ALL RIGHTS RESERVED

CAUTION: Professionals and amateurs are hereby warned that *ODD* is subject to a Licensing Fee. It is fully protected under the copyright laws of the United States of America, the British Commonwealth, including Canada, and all other countries of the Copyright Union. All rights, including professional, amateur, motion picture, recitation, lecturing, public reading, radio broadcasting, television and the rights of translation into foreign languages are strictly reserved. In its present form the play is dedicated to the reading public only.

The amateur live stage performance rights to *ODD* are controlled exclusively by Samuel French, Inc., and licensing arrangements and performance licenses must be secured well in advance of presentation. PLEASE NOTE that amateur Licensing Fees are set upon application in accordance with your producing circumstances. When applying for a licensing quotation and a performance license please give us the number of performances intended, dates of production, your seating capacity and admission fee. Licensing Fees are payable one week before the opening performance of the play to Samuel French, Inc., at 45 W. 25th Street, New York, NY 10010.

Licensing Fee of the required amount must be paid whether the play is presented for charity or gain and whether or not admission is charged.

Stock licensing fees quoted upon application to Samuel French, Inc.

For all other rights than those stipulated above, apply to: Barbara Hogenson Agency, Inc., 215 West 92nd Street, Suite 15G, New York, NY 10025.

Particular emphasis is laid on the question of amateur or professional readings, permission and terms for which must be secured in writing from Samuel French, Inc.

Copying from this book in whole or in part is strictly forbidden by law, and the right of performance is not transferable.

Whenever the play is produced the following notice must appear on all programs, printing and advertising for the play: "Produced by special arrangement with Samuel French, Inc."

Due authorship credit must be given on all programs, printing and advertising for the play.

ISBN 978-0-573-69728-9   Printed in U.S.A.   #29108

No one shall commit or authorize any act or omission by which the copyright of, or the right to copyright, this play may be impaired.

No one shall make any changes in this play for the purpose of production.

Publication of this play does not imply availability for performance. Both amateurs and professionals considering a production are strongly advised in their own interests to apply to Samuel French, Inc., for written permission before starting rehearsals, advertising, or booking a theatre.

No part of this book may be reproduced, stored in a retrieval system, or transmitted in any form, by any means, now known or yet to be invented, including mechanical, electronic, photocopying, recording, videotaping, or otherwise, without the prior written permission of the publisher.

MUSIC USE NOTE

Licensees are solely responsible for obtaining formal written permission from copyright owners to use copyrighted music in the performance of this play and are strongly cautioned to do so. If no such permission is obtained by the licensee, then the licensee must use only original music that the licensee owns and controls. Licensees are solely responsible and liable for all music clearances and shall indemnify the copyright owners of the play and their licensing agent, Samuel French, Inc., against any costs, expenses, losses and liabilities arising from the use of music by licensees.

IMPORTANT BILLING AND CREDIT REQUIREMENTS

All producers of *ODD must* give credit to the Author of the Play in all programs distributed in connection with performances of the Play, and in all instances in which the title of the Play appears for the purposes of advertising, publicizing or otherwise exploiting the Play and/or a production. The name of the Author *must* appear on a separate line on which no other name appears, immediately following the title and *must* appear in size of type not less than fifty percent of the size of the title type.

In addition the following credit *must* be given in all programs and publicity information distributed in association with this piece:

Originally produced by Premiere Stages
At Kean University
Union, New Jersey
John Wooten, Producing Artistic Director

ODD had its world premiere at Premiere Stages, in a joint production with Kean University (John Wooten, Producing Artistic Director) on September 7, 2007. The scenic design was by Joseph M. Gourley, lighting design by Nadine Charlsen, costumes by Ingrid Proos, and sound by Bryan Pekarek. The dramaturg was Elizabeth Coen, the Production Stage Manager was Danny Douress, and the direction was by John Wooten, with the following cast:

MICAH DONATO	Malachy Orozco
ANNA MARIE DONATO	Toby Poser
JOE ESKIN	Joseph Adams
ILONA LAWLER	Ilana Seagull

ODD was the winner of the 2007 Premiere Stages Play Festival.

THE CHARACTERS

MICAH – 15; wounded and raging, cynical and untrusting; yet with lucid glimmers of vulnerability and on rare occasions, even a sense of wonder.

JOE – 40s; an enigmatic loner, not without charisma; straightforward and compassionate but at times impatient, intermittently inaccessible, and prone to flashes of hostility.

ANNA MARIE – 40s, Micah's mother; wan, palpably beleaguered, and classically battle-fatigued from the parenting wars; defensively edgy but aching for a gentler existence.

ILONA – 17; Micah's peer tutor, aggressively ambitious and self-possessed; though both sharp and sharp-tongued, genuinely responsive to tenderness.

THE SETTING

In and around Mount Morris, New Jersey.

THE TIME

Now. September to November.

For rigorous teachers seized my youth,
And purged its faith, and trimmed its fire,
Showed me the high, white star of truth,
There bade me gaze, and there aspire.
          Matthew Arnold

Memory flung up in him the primitive thoughts
which are youth's inheritance, but which with him
had remained latent, never leaping up into a blaze.
          Thomas Mann, *Death in Venice*

ACT ONE

1.

(In-your-face punk rock plays in the blackness. A light picks up: a teenaged boy, stretched across a worn picnic table. As lights rise around him, we're in Mount Morris, New Jersey, the backyard of a pre-war duplex. A sultry afternoon in September, as suffocating as any in midsummer. **MICAH DONATO** *is fifteen, wears stained cutoff cargo pants, no shoes. His face and torso are streaked, his hair matted. He's eating gourmet cookies, frosting melting messily on his fingers and face, and to the accompaniment of driving music spilling from his boom box, aggressively playing a Game Boy taped together with blackened masking tape.)*

*(***MICAH*** pauses, grabs the cookie box to check out some ingredient, then drops it back on the table and resumes his mini video game.)*

*(***ANNA MARIE DONATO*** enters, accompanying* **JOE ESKIN***; both are in their 40s.* **ANNA MARIE** *turns off the boom box.)*

MICAH. Now what. So who's *this*.

JOE. You didn't tell him?

MICAH. "Tell me" *what*.

JOE. I was coming?

MICAH. Coming for what? Who *is* this, a shrink, 'cop?

ANNA MARIE. Hand me that game thing.

MICAH. My father?

> *(***ANNA MARIE*** snatches the Game Boy.)*
>
> Gimme that!

(**MICAH** *would wrestle it from her, but* **ANNA MARIE** *slides it in her bag, strategically drops her bag to the ground and puts her foot on it.* **MICAH** *mock punches her face, accompanied by a loud Kung Fu-styled shriek, then reaching for another cookie, glances again back at* **JOE**:)

JOE. I'm not your father.

ANNA MARIE. Meet your new English tutor. Mr. Joe Eskin.

JOE. *(offering hand)* Micah.

MICAH. Where'd ya find *him*?

ANNA MARIE. He just moved up here from Asbury Park. Put up flyers. Lives a few blocks over, 'other side of the pond, on Oldwick.

MICAH. "Flyers?" Loser.

JOE. Shake my hand, Micah? Please?

(**MICAH** *starts to, gives him the finger instead.*)

What are those, cookies?

MICAH. Yeah, Bahlsen Waffelettens and you can't have any, they're all –

(suddenly, up in his face)

MIIIIINE. Here! Well, *HEEEERE* –

JOE. *(over)* Don't do that. I'll pass. – DON'T DO THAT. 'Look a little gooey.

MICAH. Humidity. Don'tcha even wanna *lick*?

JOE. You got 'em all over your face. And apparently not just the current box. Looked in a mirror lately?

ANNA MARIE. Micah's not a big fan of mirrors.

(examines the cookie box)

From Germany, sure. Take money outta my pants pocket for these when I was showering? A five's missing.

MICAH. About all five bucks buys in this town.

ANNA MARIE. Not all.

MICAH. 'Fraid I won't "D.A.R.E. To Say No." You 'been listening to that dumb Jamaican bitch at the hospital.

JOE. Shouldn't speak that way about women, 'specially round your mom.

MICAH. 'S not like I called *her* a bitch. *Today.*

ANNA MARIE. Did you skip lunch? You took your thing this morning, I saw.

MICAH. "Thing?" Meds, *meds*, MEDS. Kinda late to get all, like, ashamed.

ANNA MARIE. Your appetite. You're not spitting it in the toilet again, are you?

MICAH. You stupid idiot, don'tcha even remember 'bout SR? Wears off.

JOE. Which meds are these?

ANNA MARIE. After a few weeks off in August, we go back on our old standby. We tried Cylert and Dexedrine, and the year before what was it – Imipramine?

MICAH. *(over)* – *And,* you *stupid* idi – then? – hel*lo*? – *Clonidine.*

JOE. Don't call your mother stupid. And "the old standby" *is*?

MICAH. Ritalin, SR. 'Keeps me from bouncin' off the ceiling AND KILLING HER.

ANNA MARIE. "S.R., sustai –

MICAH. *(over)* – SUSTAINED RELEASE." One big fat twenty, steada' two tens –

ANNA MARIE. *(over)* Ten milligrams. Of methylphenidate, the generic. Two doses are supposed to work better, but –

MICAH. 'Nurse at school has to give me one –

ANNA MARIE. *(over)* 'Old fashioned type, doesn't believe in psychotropics –

MICAH. *(over)* LET *ME* EXPLAIN. IT'S MY BODY. She goes, "I don't see what good these do kids like *you*," and I go, "Well *eat* me, Lady, 'cause nicotine's a drug, too, you *addict*, with your black teeth and Newport breath, and it don't do shit for your personality problem."

ANNA MARIE. He doesn't sleep so good with a extra daytime pill, and got lunch this year at one thirty.

JOE. I hear when you get to dose yourself, you can sell that stuff on the playground.

MICAH. Playgrounds are where ya score weed. I 'been on mind-altering shit forever and don't need anything extra to make me sociable. How much 'he charge?

JOE. Twenty-five. – And are you? "Sociable?" Coulda' fooled me.

MICAH. Yeah and you're a loser. Even queers over in Maplewood get forty.

(to ANNA MARIE)

'Guess losers over on Oldwick…are even poorer than a loser like you.

JOE. Your mother lets you speak to her that way?

ANNA MARIE. I choose my battles.

MICAH. Why 'you so cheap, loser?

JOE. Don't call me that. 'Cause I'm new to the area. Got no track record.

ANNA MARIE. And since he's more affordable, he can come more than once a week.

MICAH. If you think I'm your guinea pig, you're whacked.

JOE. Just tell me why you don't bathe. In this heat, even standing a few feet away, you're about a half hour from drawing flies.

MICAH. Tell him how, like, *condemned* our bathroom is. Way small, chipped tub, smelly water 'has to run a hour to get the shit color out. Some days, I skip it.

JOE. Get any feedback on this hygiene problem? Other kids move away from you in the lunch room?

MICAH. Not 'cause I stink.

ANNA MARIE. Micah doesn't like the feeling of a shower, of being –

MICAH. "Encloooooosed."

(sci-fi theme, up in JOE's face)

Duh-duh-*duh*-duh-duh-duh *duh*-duh – ahhhhhhhHH HHHH –

JOE. *(over)* Don't do that. *Don't.* Didn't you hear me, STOP IT.

ANNA MARIE. MICAH.

(MICAH wheels around, screams in her face.)

ANNA MARIE. I have to buy clear shower curtains, so he can see out.

MICAH. I get claustrophob*ic*. 'Cause I got claustrophob*ia*.

JOE. You sound proud. Guess solitary confinement's out, as a discipline option.

MICAH. Think you're gonna, like, "get through to me, using humor"?

ANNA MARIE. He's gonna help you with your reading, your English work.

JOE. But we definitely won't start today. I don't want to get that close.

MICAH. Haven't you heard? By tenth grade, it's too late for Sped kids –

ANNA MARIE. *(over)* – Special Ed.

MICAH. *(over)* – Nurse Buttface says so. In *our* brains, when the glob a' gray puss finally got hard, the neutrons got smushed together wrong so we can't learn shit.

JOE. But you kinda like that distinction, diagnosed a lost cause.

MICAH. And *you* kinda like me being, like, "a challenge?"

JOE. I hate challenges, I just need cash and don't have a mom handy to steal from.

ANNA MARIE. We agreed to try a coupla sessions as a trial.

MICAH. Need fifty bucks that bad?

JOE. I'm not in it for the thrill of spending two hours with a teenager.

MICAH. You don't like kids?

JOE. And forget just how much, 'til a moment like this.

MICAH. *(mock reaction, as if kicked in solar plexus)* Ohhh. You hang out in New York?

JOE. Only when I can afford it.

MICAH. Which must be never. *She* won't let me.

JOE. Clearly, she's got good reason to chain you to your bed.

MICAH. Watch out! "Comedy!"

(**JOE** *pulls out a small spiral notebook:*)

JOE. Here. 'Til next time, take this.

MICAH. What, like, a cherry lollipop from the barber?

JOE. Nope, I don't do rewards. Carry it. Scribble something when you feel – claustrophobic. Play tick-tack-toe, make lists of scatological words for people who piss ya off.

(*With his chocolate thumb,* **MICAH** *makes a print on a page; rips it out, drops it on the ground.*)

Or don't. Suit yourself.

MICAH. Next time I'll shower n' wear perfume, just for you. You a queer?

ANNA MARIE. *MICAH.*

JOE. Are you?

MICAH. Ask her, I'm just a bad-ass with anger issues.

(*He starts off, looks back, suspicious, goes.* **JOE** *takes out a bottle, shakes a pill in his mouth.*)

ANNA MARIE. You're on medication?

JOE. "Too?" Nope, just Ibuprofen. Generic's cheaper, like Ritalin. *Well.* 'Certainly looks healthy, anyway. For a boy who lives on crap.

ANNA MARIE. I hope you could see how – how *underneath*, Micah has a sharp mind.

JOE. 'Cause he curses precisely? I don't put that much stock in sharp.

ANNA MARIE. Then what *do* you put stock in? I'm sorry, you say you need the money, but you barely even tried to win him over.

JOE. Why should I have to win over a little snot like that? What's that teach him? I'm not Mr. Rogers. I don't stroke people. 'Specially not a punk kid as rude and apparently spoiled as that one.

ANNA MARIE. HE'S NOT SPOILED.

MICAH. *(off) (yelling in:)* Our TV's so fuckin' ancient, like, half the buttons are broke off. Won't even turn *on* without the remote! SO WHERE IS IT?

ANNA MARIE. WHEREVER YOU LEFT IT!

JOE. Was he ever...any kinder, to you?

ANNA MARIE. An adorable little thing who gave Mommy a valentine in Kindergarten?

JOE. Never stole you a big heart shaped box of chocolates?

ANNA MARIE. Even though they told me early on about the attention thing, and being borderline L.D. – learning disabled – it wasn't 'til 'coupla years ago they officially diagnosed his other problem.

JOE. Nonstop hostility towards the world.

ANNA MARIE. 'Specially me. "O.D.D." Oppositional Defiant Disorder.

JOE. Why you choose your battles.

ANNA MARIE. Drugs don't really treat that, though the Clonidine was supposed to take the edge off. But he's easier to take when he's not going off in forty directions.

JOE. Ever wanna skip the pricey pharmaceuticals and just clobber him?

ANNA MARIE. Beat him? I'd never, ev –

JOE. *(over)* – 'Must get tempted.

ANNA MARIE. I put walls between us instead. But if I lock him in his room, he just takes the door off the hinges with a screwdriver. Stays up all night watching the food channel, then screams at me to order some useless kitchen equipment, sushi knives, an electric sandwich maker...

JOE. "Only three payments of 19.95." Least he's interested in something.

ANNA MARIE. No, he's not. It's just another distraction, no different from blasting cartoons at five a.m. or banging the toilet like a drum 'til it breaks, just another way to *get* me, to wreck a night's sleep. And when I don't promise to buy the junk, he has a tantrum. Leaps up n' down –

JOE. – Sprains his ankles all the time.

ANNA MARIE. Jumping off furniture – *yeah* – How'd you know? I used to wanna get rid of the TV. I hid it once. But I missed it too much. I mean, it's all we have.

JOE. What else do you do for fun?

MICAH. *(off)* Fuck...

ANNA MARIE. Do I look like a woman who has fun?

MICAH. *(off)* ...Fuck. Fuck. Fuck.

JOE. By the way, what's with the name, "Micah?"

ANNA MARIE. Didn't sound Italian. Like kids 'this side of town. I thought if I gave him a special name, he'd turn out special...

MICAH. *(off)* Fuck! 'S almost time for "Unwrapped!" WHERE *IS* IT?

ANNA MARIE. ...One of the million things I was wrong about.

(**ANNA MARIE** *goes.* **JOE** *picks up the smeared notebook page, pockets it. Lights fade, then rise on* **MICAH**, *cleaned-up considerably.*)

2.

(As **JOE** *joins him, in: the Donato living room.*)

MICAH. I'm not, like, in the *mood,* and you're way early.

JOE. Nope, you're late. Forty-one minutes, so we have only nineteen left.

MICAH. No WAAAAAAAAY –

JOE. Stop that. I told you, do not get up in my face.

MICAH. *(taunting, in his face:)* Why NOT, 'least I'm... Spankin' CLEAN. Bought Coast soap, just for YOOOUUU –

JOE. *STOP.* No reason to get a gold star.

MICAH. I never got no gold stars.

JOE. I'm sure you didn't.

MICAH. You're a real dick. My mom wouldn't like how you talk to me.

JOE. She can fire me, any time. Now pull out something and read it out loud.

MICAH. I didn't bring a book home. Sped kids don't get, like, regular homework. Only gotta read in class. And *we* still move our lips. We're pathetic.

(**JOE** *rummages in* **MICAH**'s *backpack, finds the spiral notebook.*)

JOE. Some personalized hieroglyphics. Beats blank pages. Keep it up.

(**MICAH** *throws it over.* **JOE** *throws it back at him.*)

MICAH. WATCH IT. Don't ya think it's weird we don't have a computer?

JOE. Nope, probably not safe 'round you.

MICAH. Had one, *used* piece a' shit. Ugly monitor, like, way big. No internet.

JOE. So you demolished it with a baseball bat.

MICAH. 'Peed on it one night.

JOE. To piss off Mom. Or just 'cause ya had to piss?

MICAH. (*shocked* **JOE**'s *intuited the truth*) *Yeah*, Man, totally half-asleep – Mom says you write, like, "stories" or some lame shit. What the fuck about?

JOE. None of your damned business.

MICAH. *Ooooh.* 'Use a little fairy-size notebook computer?

JOE. Nope, write by hand, 'way I'm teaching you to.

MICAH. "Personalized hieroglyph-shit?" Lo-*ser.*

JOE. Don't call me that again. Here, focus, then read me some of this.

(**JOE** *takes out a paperback* Robinson Crusoe.)

MICAH. You gotta be fuckin' kid – "Robin's *son* Cru – *so*

– ee." And it *smells*.

JOE. A lady was selling off stuff on an old quilt by the train station. Cost a quarter. We got eighteen minutes. I want to see if you can sit still.

MICAH. NO. *Asshole*.

JOE. Then we'll just sit. Seventeen and a half more minutes. And do not call me asshole again, *asshole*.

MICAH. Aren't ya worried how this looks? Like, on a *loveseat* with me, no mom home?

JOE. Nope, yours pays me to sit next to you, wherever the hell I want.

MICAH. What if my mom's got a secret camera, recording you cursing at me. We could sue your ass.

JOE. A hospital billing clerk with a crumbling bathroom doesn't have state-of-the-art surveillance equipment. And I don't have a cent to collect. Which is why you'd better not even think about stealing from *me*. Now sit. Or squat on the floor. Or stand. I don't care, 'long as you're completely still.

(**MICAH** *flips* Robinson Crusoe *open, halfway.*)

Focus. For now, on "*The Life and Strange Surprising Adventures…*"

(**MICAH** *grabs the spiral notebook again.*)

MICAH. Maybe I'll write weird violent shit in here – like, how I wanna shove, like, nitroglyceride up the my Sped teacher's pussy n'blow her to Newark. And they'll find it, and I'll be all, like, "HIM! He made me write it!"

JOE. Do that. But for the next sixteen minutes, don't speak a word that isn't printed on that page. And it's nitroglyce*rine*.

MICAH. "…The…the poor cr-creature was a comely h-hansome fellow, perfectly well made; with st-straight strong limbs, not too large; tall and well shaped – THIS IS TOTAL HOMO SHIT.

JOE. LISTEN UP: The next guy your mom brings in will be even worse, some humorless Marine who got his nuts blown off, with a grudge against kids who don't plan to join up and become a real man like him. So appreciate how comparatively *easy* I am. Sit up straight, for once don't think about how pissed you are. Focus on these words only, even if they mean zip to you.

MICAH. *(tense beat, then:)* "…And…as I r-reckon, about twenty-six years of age." What's "reckon"?

JOE. To evaluate, form an opinion. As in, "I reckon you're not the filthy slob I thought you were the first time I smelled you."

(MICAH remains suspicious. As lights fade, MICAH reads further from Robinson Crusoe*:)*

MICAH. "…At last he lays his head flat upon the ground, close to my foot, and sets my other foot upon his head…and made all the signs to me of subjection, servitude, and submission imaginable, to let me know how he would serve me as long as he lived…"

(A flash of lightning. **ANNA MARIE** *appears:)*

3.

(Edge of a local pond. Late afternoon. Distant thunder. Wilted **ANNA MARIE** *fans herself, nervously looks over the water as* **JOE** *arrives.)*

JOE. Storm's about to blow in, over the mountaintop. Here we are, next to water. Such as it is. "Feoli Pond." More like a puddle.

ANNA MARIE. Funny you should call it that. My Nonna always said it's nothing but a *pozza* – "*pozza*" – puddle. When I was a kid, 'cause it's in the eastern part of town, they called it "Wop Lake."

JOE. You Wops afraid of lightning?

ANNA MARIE. I sorta admire it. You can't control it, 'just shows up. But I'm glad it's finally September. I hate summer.

JOE. 'Cause Micah's home, all day, every day.

ANNA MARIE. Watching loud TV, eating sweets til midnight. Do you know there's actually a *Food* show called "Sugar Rush?"

JOE. But he somehow stays lean n' mean. Even off the drug?

ANNA MARIE. A.D.D.-ers just don't gain. I always think when he goes back to school, it'll be different, not just that he won't eat so much crap. That *he'll* be –

(*Lightning flashes.* **ANNA MARIE** *looks up at the sky. Thunder rumbles, distant.*)

JOE. A whole different kid, still lean, not so mean?

ANNA MARIE. Back on his meds, they'll make him brand new. 'Time I stopped *that* –

JOE. *(over)* Okay, so get to the bad news. How bad's the bitching? About me?

ANNA MARIE. Oh no, no – Micah barely mentions you.

JOE. *What?* Come on. He's gotta. I mean – isn't that why we're here?

ANNA MARIE. No, no – I – I keep waiting for *you* to call *me*. With – complaints.

JOE. So – what? – you asked me here to give me a chance to *quit*?

ANNA MARIE. I *asked* you to find out if you've done anything at all to help my son!

JOE. *(beat)* I dunno, we haven't even gotten to…to comprehension or grammar. I just wanna get him to do a single thing the *instant* someone asks him to.

ANNA MARIE. To break his will? Good luck, nobody else has. I've started to wonder if he could ever even hold a job at that car wash down there.

JOE. And it all goes back to you. Attention deficit, the defiance thing, all your fault. Mom screwed up somehow, kid got damaged, usual end of story?

ANNA MARIE. Don't play psychiatrist with me. 'Think you're the first to try –

JOE. *(over)* No, in fact – I've only seen you twice, and you seem –

ANNA MARIE. Guilty? WELL, I'M NOT.

JOE. *Hey.* I was just gonna say: over-analyzed.

(**ANNA MARIE**'s *cell rings; agitated* **MICAH** *appears with a bowl and spoon, wearing a long, battered chef's apron:*)

ANNA MARIE. What's happened now?

MICAH. Where's all my puddings, my individual Swiss Miss vanilla *snack* cups?

ANNA MARIE. Didn't buy any.

MICAH. Why not, 'told ya we were *out,* twice!

ANNA MARIE. They're for kids' lunchboxes, you're too old for –

MICAH. – NO, I'M NOT – I was gonna combine 'em and, like, float 'em in some – aw, you'd never get it – then I'm gonna fix something else instead –

ANNA MARIE. *(over)* I'll be home soon to make dinner, don't mess up the kitch –

MICAH. *(over)* – Hey, where's my box a' mocha chocolate mousse mix from Canada, 'used to be on the top shelf? I bought that one time at the Kings with my own money!

ANNA MARIE. Mousse – I threw that out, it was two years ol –

MICAH. *(over)* Then I'm making something from scratch – we still got that marshmallow shit in a jar, where'd ya hide that? – And that old double boiler?

ANNA MARIE. 'Told you, the handle was loose, you could spill –

MICAH. – I'm not gonna set myself on fire. You just don't want me to have any interests, you think I can't do anything. WATCH, I'll be famous someday on *Food* and when everybody *else* is, all, like, "I learned watching my mom make homemade *gnocchi*," I'll go, "*My* mom was a fuckin' cop who locked up her beat-up pans to keep me from learning *shit.*"

(He hangs up; **ANNA MARIE** *switches off her cell.)*

ANNA MARIE. Some say he's "hardwired" the way he is. I don't know if I even believe it. Was it 'cause I drank a margarita before I knew I was carrying him? Or he was born only four pounds? Or ate poison paint chips off the wall?

(a weary, cynical shrug)

I keep biting the inside of my mouth, til I get a blood blister and have to put ice chips on it. This old wives' tale says that's 'cause I'm scared to say something, out loud.

JOE. Or you just eat too fast, to get done before Micah. Try chewing slowly.

ANNA MARIE. I'm no good at slow. People at the hospital laugh about how fast I walk. And if I'm hit by an SUV someday, then what'll happen? Some stranger would get him who'd be…blank. Maybe there'd be this miracle, this new person would see him different, so he'd turn into a different kid.

JOE. Not family?

ANNA MARIE. No family's left. He'd end up with somebody paid by Jersey.

JOE. If I were nosy, I'd ask about his father.

ANNA MARIE. But you won't, 'cause you're not really a curious man.

JOE. *(small smile)* Micah keeps ranting about seeing New York. Ever try to run away?

ANNA MARIE. Him or me? When he was eleven he jumped on a train in a spring blizzard and got as far as Peapack before a lady conductor called me. It was crowded, no seats. And when the snow hit the windows, Micah couldn't see out, felt trapped.

JOE. Like with the shower curtain.

ANNA MARIE. And when I got there, he was pitchin' snowballs at the station windows. Threw a packed ice ball at my head that almost gave me a concussion. When we got home, I couldn't stop thinking, what if he *had* – run away.

(More lightning. **JOE** *stretches his legs.)*

JOE. Gotta move on to the Sea Catch. The AARP crowd piles up at five.

ANNA MARIE. For the sunset bargain dinner.

JOE. 'Literally line up in the parking lot, eyes trained on the door, checking their watches. It's grim.

ANNA MARIE. For a wedge a' iceberg, with a glop of blue cheese.

JOE. Then three ounces of dry grouper, $8.99.

ANNA MARIE. And some dangerous looking rice pudding.

JOE. Which they demand and never eat.

ANNA MARIE. Like old people in my hospital cafeteria. They look so disappointed in whatever they take, the minute it's on their tray…

JOE. But terrified to put it back, 'cause somebody else might get it.

ANNA MARIE. Y'know…me n' this girl I work with – she's crazy about fried calamari, even the chewy kind 'pulls fillings outta your teeth – we could come in your place some time. Give ya a break from waiting on old-timers.

JOE. Don't. Ever. The lighting alone will kill your appetite.

(She looks away, stung; an olive branch:)

But…we could compare our…geriatric phobias on more…private turf.

ANNA MARIE. More private, how?

JOE. I dunno, 'least someplace darker…maybe with a drink?

ANNA MARIE. 'Buy me a coupla Chardonnays? Get me to "open up?" 'Think all I need's to be treated good by a nice man –

JOE. Whoa. Hey. *Hey.* I'm not that nice. I've been described as emotionally autistic by more than one woman. Tell Micah he better be on time.

(Electrical flash. **JOE** *goes.* **ANNA MARIE** *starts to stop him; halts – regretful. Thunder. Lights fade.* **MICAH** *appears, reads* Crusoe *with an affected accent:)*

MICAH. "…I let him know I was very well pleased with him; in a little time, I began to teach him to speak to me… and first, I made him know his name should be Friday, which was the day I saved his life…"

4.

(The Donato living room and later yard. **MICAH** *slams* Crusoe *shut, grabs a nail clipper.)*

JOE. You read better British. Gives you something else to zero in on.

*(***MICAH*** throws down the book, trims toenails:)*

Don't do that. Hey. *HEY.* Don't..

MICAH. My house. And you're always bitchin' at me to clean up.

JOE. But I don't want to watch. I said, knock it off –

MICAH. *(over)* – So get the fuck out, Man. We're way done. Like, *GO*.

*(***MICAH*** lies back, brazenly sticks a bare foot right in* **JOE***'s face.* **JOE** *shoves it away, hard.)*

JOE. Can't. Your mom and I are grabbing a beer up the street.

MICAH. What, like, a *date*? My mom? Think she's gonna suck your dick or something?

JOE. I haven't thought that far ahead. But there's really no comfortable spot to manage it. You here, with your toenails and behavior issues, me more or less a boarder at my place. With no privacy, 'seems unlikely.

MICAH. Yeah, but if you buy her a beer again on Friday and go, "Let's take a walk by the pond!" and, like, squeeze her tit? Then, two weeks from now, you can have, like, all-you-can-eat Chinese and bone her in your back seat.

JOE. Car sex after Kung Po chicken. Pretty grim romantic fantasy.

(Jabbing **JOE** *again with his foot, taunting:)*

MICAH. Sure ya couldn't do it here, with me in my room? If I promise I won't listen?

(again jabbing his foot at JOE)

You could turn the TV way up, so I don't hear. You'd be, like, *"Ya like that? DO ya? THAT!"* And she'd go, *"Oh, Joooooeee – "*

(Jabs his foot again. JOE grabs it, harder. MICAH tries to wriggle it away but JOE holds it, firm.)

MICAH. *(cont.)* – Ow – *owww* – hey – heeeey! That HURTS*!* Fuck, stop, Man – STOOOP*!*

(JOE finally releases his foot; MICAH rubs it)

Shit. *Man.* One problem with your "date." *My* mom don't *get* laid.

JOE. Must've at least once, or you wouldn't be here to raise the provocative topic.

(notices a pink 4 x 6 index card inserted in Crusoe*)*

Who's – "Ilona?"

MICAH. This, like, math-geek skank 'school's making me call. Since I need "help" in everything 'cept lunch. My toe *HURTS*, y'know that!

JOE. – "I-lon-a." Exotic name. And she squirted perfume on her card.

ANNA MARIE. *(entering)* Sorry, my bus was late, and packed.

MICAH. *That's* why kids dis me. Not 'cause I'm Sped, 'cause *she* rides the bus like a Costa Rican to save gas. – Is that make-up shit on your eyes? To try to look like a regular woman?

JOE. Nobody solicited your opinion.

MICAH. Nobody asked you to show up with a hard-on for my mom.

ANNA MARIE. Micah *Donato*! Be quiet or I'll flush those Peroggina things you stole down the toilet.

(They start out, into the yard; MICAH follows.)

MICAH. Wherever you two are goin', I'M COMIN', TOO.

JOE. No you're not.

ANNA MARIE. Micah, you always beg me to leave you alone –

MICAH. *(coming outside)* I'M C*OMIN' TONIGHT.*

JOE. Want to take that down a notch, immediately?

*(***ANNA MARIE** *and* **JOE** *continue on.)*

ANNA MARIE. If you close the windows, you can blast the TV 'loud as you want. We got macaroni to microwave, that salty kind you like.

MICAH. Not anymore I don't. It's crap poor people buy with food stamps. – MOM. *MOM.* HE TRIED TO FOOL WITH ME.

*(***ANNA MARIE** *and* **JOE** *stop.)*

Just now. Grabbed me, in a weirdo way.

JOE. You, Mr. Wierdo, stuck your dirty foot in my face. Twice.

MICAH. And you loved it, 'til you almost yanked my toe off. It may be fuckin' *broke!*

ANNA MARIE. Did you forget your pill today?

MICAH. You fuckin' *phony.* Look at you. Some guy shows up, and you, like, start acting like you're playin' the *part* of a mom.

*(***MICAH** *retreats.* **JOE** *follows, shoving* **MICAH** *in a chair, almost knocking the wind out of him:)*

JOE. And what the hell are you playing! Grab your notebook and get centered.

(As **JOE** *rejoins* **ANNA MARIE***,* **MICAH** *grabs his notebook, then jumps up and calls off:)*

MICAH. HEY! I COULD WRITE TWISTED SHIT 'GETS YOU *ARRESTED.*

(He grabs the clipper, uses it to aggressively carve the picnic table. As lights rise on:)

5.

(A bar. An old pop recording, something like Hank Williams's "I'm So Lonesome I Could Cry" wafts in. **ANNA MARIE** and **JOE** have beers. In progress:)*

ANNA MARIE. ...Like – this morning – he pulled a toy outta the Sugar Crisp box, when he didn't know I was watching? Turned it over in his hand, like a treasure. Then I walked in, he yanked the toy's head off and threw it across the room. I said clean it up, but he just stomped on it 'til it was plastic dust and ate halfa' box of Italian ladyfingers.

JOE. Y'know, despite his indifference to hygiene, Micah knows he's attractive.

ANNA MARIE. Didn't get that from me. I have to remember to put on lipstick.

JOE. Where ya think he got it from?

*(**ANNA MARIE** falls silent.)*

Shaky ground again? I shouldn't go there?

ANNA MARIE. No you should NOT.

(nervously reconsidering: a 180)

My son...is *not*...a – "a love child."

*(beat; **JOE** just nods)*

Yeah.

(nervous sip of beer)

Later on, people asked if it was the "date kind." Like, if we'd had a couple of these and talked about the Jets before he slammed my skull against my car window,

*See Music Use Note, Page 3

it woulda' been better.

JOE. At...home this hap – ?

ANNA MARIE. *(flaring briefly)* – Course not. In – Livingston. 'Mall. After buying a wedding gift for my supervisor. 'Billing staff had a collection, picked me to shop. I got her an electric knife at Macy's. It was there, the whole time, and I kept thinking it could help me if I could just plug it in. He'd been right behind me in line at the Macy's, kinda friendly, y'know, and I guess, followed me out to my – When I saw him, I just thought I musta left something back at the register. 'Opened my door for me, so poli – And – even talked. Maybe as much as he would've on a date, so who knows? I haven't had many, can't ya tell?

JOE. Me neither. But – so afterwards, you didn't consider – *not* having – ?

ANNA MARIE. THAT'S ENOUGH ABOUT ALL THAT. Here's your hard-earned money. Forgot to pay up back at the house.

(Lights fade on them, rising on **MICAH** *and just-arrived* **ILONA**, *17 going on 35.* **MICAH** *repeatedly pounds a cushion in a marital arts-styled move, self-absorbed.* **ILONA** *watches:)*

ILONA. Well *whoa*, you're *so*, like…like not, like, my *usual.*

MICAH. You get paid for this?

ILONA. No, Babe, I generously offer all services for free.

MICAH. No way. How come?

ILONA. 'Cause I'm a wonderful person, one in a fucking million, who didn't do forensics or marching band or swim team. Got any brothers or sisters?

MICAH. Just a mom. She's a real bitch but she's totally out.

ILONA. Cool. So where 'you wanna, you know, *do* this?

MICAH. Here's good. 'Like cookies?

ILONA. *Cookies?*

MICAH. I got Midor Meringue Noisettes with chocolate hazelnut filing…Pirouline Wafer rolls…Walker Shortbread Rounds…'few Stella Doro Swiss Fudge – oh

– maybe a coupla Pepperidge Farm Marabella Toffees, but just pieces.

ILONA. You're O.C.D. or something, right? Have a photographic memory and can recite, like, all the different pasta shapes on the shelves at the grocery store? Gotta study 'em every time you're there, or you have to *go back?*

MICAH. Not O.*C* – O.*D.*, O.*D.D.*

ILONA. So sharpen up your number two pencil, odd-boy –

MICAH. – Wait – don't move.

(**MICAH** *darts off.* **ILONA** *sneaks an Absolut vodka miniature from her purse, takes a swig. Lights rise on* **JOE** *and* **ANNA MARIE**:)

ANNA MARIE. Connie, my boss, just back from her honeymoon cruise, dragged me to get it done. And she was a once-a-day mass-goer.

JOE. But you refused. Saw it as –

ANNA MARIE. – A blessing? 'Sounds good to say I put my foot down. But time'd marched on. They looked at me, these nurses over in Rahway, and go "Honey, you work in a hospital, don't you *know*? You're halfway *there*."

(beat)

Leaving the clinic, Connie started reciting The Rosary, and I hauled off and slapped her so hard it left a welt. Not a good career move, huh?

(longer swig of beer)

Another woman at work sent over a counselor. Who warned me, when I saw the baby's face, we might not "bond," the mall night would come flashing back. "Counselor?" Baby broker. She just happened to know this couple in New Providence who didn't have the cash to fly to China. I kicked her outta my house along with her pamphlets and "hotline" numbers. I hate "hotlines."

JOE. Easy answers to everything –

ANNA MARIE. – some stranger you dial up in the middle of the night –

JOE. – 'chirpy volunteer who's had too much coffee –

ANNA MARIE. – and you *know* can't wait to go home to her own life that's so perfect she'd never be caught dead calling a "hotline" herself.

JOE. But then, when Micah was born – ?

ANNA MARIE. DON'T TURN THIS INTO THE THIRD DEGREE.

(**JOE** *puts a hand up, a truce gesture.*)

I didn't see that creep in my boy's face. Micah was a jolly baby, 'started laughing before the books said he would. Is he wild 'cause I knew what he came from, and didn't pick him up enough? I picked him up. Day care people picked him up. When I'd get home, I didn't always feel like reading some cute children's book, but nobody tied him in a corner.

(**JOE** *remains silent; feeling suddenly exposed:*)

What?

JOE. It's just – you keep telling me everything you *didn't* do to him –

(**ANNA MARIE** *stands, starts to bolt.*)

Hey! Wh – whoa – whoa – *whoa* –

ANNA MARIE. *(over)* – When Micah was a toddler, he couldn't wait to see me! Used to crawl up in my lap and not wanna get down!

(**JOE** *puts up a conciliatory hand again.*)

But. Some good things have happened since. Micah found a fifty-dollar bill outside a movie theater. Let me keep ten dollars of it.

JOE. Bite your mouth tonight? Not wanting to say certain things out loud?

ANNA MARIE. No, but I don't really like beer. Or restaurants in this part of town. Even the waitresses have nicer shoes than me.

(*They start off. Piercing punk, lights up on:*)

6.

(*The Donato living room.* **ILONA**'s *straddling shirtless* **MICAH**, *hands on his chest.* **ANNA MARIE** *and* **JOE** *enter,* **ANNA MARIE** *instantly kills the boom box.* **ILONA** *slips off* **MICAH**.)

ANNA MARIE. Whoever you are, you leave my house.

MICAH. Mom, STOP, *STOP*.

| **ANNA MARIE.** | **JOE.** |
| GO – | Hey, let's hold on here – |

ANNA MARIE. *(over)* Did you hear me? Out –

MICAH. Calm down, it's just my other tutor, givin' me a tattoo.

ILONA. See? – Nothing controversial or, like, creepy Goth – just a broken heart and totally temporary. Baby shampoo and a sponge 'wash it right off.

(wipes her hand, thrusts it forward)

Uh, *Hi*. – Ilona Lawler.

JOE. With the perfumed business card.

ANNA MARIE. *Tutor?*

ILONA. Math coach, I was assigned – by our school – so check, please. Here's the paper they gave me with your incidentals. I was gonna email you at your job, but Mic called first, and I had a little, like, window of availability.

MICAH: *(to JOE; proud)* That Miatta out there's *hers*, she a *senior*, lives up on Margate Bridge.

ILONA. Really, you musta' signed up, Ms. Donato, or I couldn't be on your premises.

ANNA MARIE. But that was weeks ago and I never heard back –

ILONA. 'Cause of a "chronic shortage." Guess there's a waiting list, and not enough, like, altruistic types like me to go 'round.

MICAH. *(to JOE, sotto)* She goes, like "You got *hairs* 'round your *nipples* yet?"

ANNA MARIE. That's enough.

MICAH. No big *deal*, I just took my shirt off, to show her –

ANNA MARIE. *(over)* THAT'S ENOUGH.

ILONA. Call Mrs. Pennington, I'm certifiably gifted in math. Middle school, 'got the highest GEPA in Jersey, got an almost perfect score on my S.A.T.

JOE. And carry tattoos.

ILONA. Oh I just used one a' those to kinda break the ice 'tween Mic and me –

MICAH. Glad I showered *tonight.*

ANNA MARIE. Just leave.

JOE. Come on, Anna Marie, no harm done –

ILONA. You some sorta step-dad?

MICAH. English coach, I gotta whole *posse* of tutors.

JOE. Joe Eskin, part of Team Micah. Listen, we brought ice cream, why don't we all have some?

ILONA.	**MICAH.**
Ms. Donato, this is so, like, regrettable…	What kinda ice cream? Better not be fuckin' low fat –

ANNA MARIE. *(over)* – I'm not in the mood anymore. This is *my* house.

MICAH. MOM! *STOP.*

ANNA MARIE. *(charging outside, showing* **ILONA** *out)* Everybody just go. Starting with you.

ILONA. May I just say, Mic's very cool, told me straight up he's, you know, in "Club *Meds.*" 'Course, everybody I tutor is. It's not, like, "oooh, a *stigma.*" They'd be smarter making a list of kids who *aren't*, right? By the way, some are into, like, writing all over themselves, you know, the answers? But since I got a peek at your son? Clean as a whistle.

MICAH. *(flashes his chest; sotto)* And I do have hairs, 'round my –

ANNA MARIE. *(over)* – Button up that shirt! And don't say another word.

JOE.	**ANNA MARIE.**
Anna Marie, nothing all that terrible went down –	And go to your room. NOW. WE'RE THROUGH. Now *goodnight.*

*(***ANNA MARIE*** shoves ***MICAH*** off, hard.)*

MICAH. *(off)* YOU MEAN *BITCH*, I NEVER GET TO HAVE *ANY FUN!*

(In the yard, **JOE** *watches* **ILONA**:*)*

ILONA. Well, *that* was harsh. Maybe *her* meds need adjusting.

JOE. Want some feedback? You didn't handle that as well as you might've.

ILONA. What the – When I got here, that boy was totally wigging, bouncin' off the fuckin' ceil –

JOE. *(over)* – I'm sure he was. I'm just saying, with Micah's *mom*, too much information might've been volunteered. Less coulda' been more.

ILONA. So you're into her? What, you two started going out, then, like, decided to tutor her kid? To, like, score some kinda point?

JOE. Other way around, actually. And I – we're not really "going – " Did you – like Micah? For real? For a – "Sped?"

ILONA. Oooh, into the lingo are we?

JOE. Come on, 'whole tattoo thing? With a kid like him?

ILONA. 'Scuse me, I'm not, like, Miss Easy Sleazy with her travelling bag a' skanky tricks, cruising the 7-11 for skateboarders –

JOE. You can give the high moral ground a rest. Around me. 'Guess everybody takes a breather from his own tribe.

ILONA. *(more than enough of him)* Right. *Listen.* Gotta go, Mister Joe. Sorry you got thrown out, too. You looked ready to cry 'bout no ice cream.

(As **ILONA** *heads off.* **JOE** *watches her. Lights fade.* **MICAH***'s voice wafts in, as lights rise on:)*

7.

(The backyard. **MICAH** *still reads haltingly, but with slightly more fluency:)*

MICAH. "For never man had a more faithful, loving, sincere servant than Friday was to me…his very affections were tied to me, like those of a child to a father."

JOE. 'Your mom say anything about the other night? Still pissed about that girl – what's her name? Ilona? Talk to her at school?

MICAH. She wouldn't say shit to me *there*. She'd be totally dissed.

JOE. I thought she was cool…as in…refreshingly blunt. And didn't seem self-conscious about our walking in on –

MICAH. *(over)* – Lemme finish reading n' get it over with –

JOE. *(over)* – I thought the *rest* of us were a little uncool. 'Your mom tell you not to see her again? Big scene, big warning about not screwing around? She's gotta right to worry.

MICAH. Why 'you so interested? Trying to be, like –

(flips open Robinson Crusoe)

– "his very affections were tied to me, like those of a child to a father – "

JOE. *(over)* – I just thought the girl was sharp. Worth getting to know. *Better*. Come on, she seemed to genuinely find *you* cool. 'Notice?

(MICAH *raises his shirt, touches his chest. The tattoo is still there, but partially peeled off.)*

MICAH. Yeah, she's "freshly blunt" all right. 'Said something kinda *weird*.

JOE. How so?

MICAH. Let's just go back to ol Cruuuusoe n' Friiiiida –

JOE. *(over)* – Are you meeting her later? Come on, what'd she say to you?

MICAH. *(touching tattoo remnant)* While she was *doin'* this, she goes, like…like…"If your – if *this* is *this* smooth, then your ass's gotta be whip cream."

JOE. Not exactly Keats, but – did you let her find out?

MICAH. Right after, you n' mom came home. Let's get *done* –

(picks up Crusoe; **JOE** *pulls it from his hands.)*

JOE. HEY! A girl's actually semi-interested in you. Acknowledge the damn win. You don't have that many friends to blow one off.

MICAH. I'm winning way more n' *you.* With your sore knees and lame dates with my bitch mom. But 'Lona couldn't hang out today.

JOE. Meet her at the pond. Women are transformed 'round bodies of water, and it's free. She's clearly very bright. Talk to her. Ask her things.

MICAH. "Ask her thi" – 'The fuck? Like, about what?

JOE. The list of stuff you don't know shit about yet. Pretend to listen closely, even if you get bored. A "focusing" skill that'll serve ya well, with or without A.D.D. Still using your notebook?

MICAH. Yep. See? *"Whip cream."* 'Bout fifty times. Thanks, m'man Friday.

(**JOE** *tosses him the* Crusoe, *watches him go. As lights shift,* **ILONA** *appears, laughing, racing into:*)

8.

(*By the pond.* **MICAH** *chases her, then catches up, grabs her and kisses her, too hard. Pushing him back,* **ILONA** *comes up for air.*)

ILONA. *Way* too much *tongue.* And all that spit, what's up with *that*?

MICAH. 'Fraid I was dry.

ILONA. You open too wide. It's not, like, CPR. Blowin' air into some old fat fuck havin' a heart attac –

MICAH. *(over)* I know what CPR is.

ILONA. You do have truly sweet breath, though. Big surprise –

(**MICAH** *grabs her, kisses her again*)

Um – better, better, but what's that shit smeared on your mouth, Chapstick?

MICAH. "Very Berry."

ILONA. Doesn't work, a guy's lips all fruity. And yours *so* don't need it.

MICAH. I don't know that stuff. Coach me – I need, like, lessons –

(**MICAH** *tries to kiss her again:*)

ILONA. Down, boy, down. Some geek's been spying on us, 'cross the pond.

MICAH. Nobody 'there now. Still wanna see my "whip cream."

(*pulls up his windbreaker, shows skin*)

ILONA. You can be a manipulative little shit, y'know that?

MICAH. Not whatcha expect, from a Sped?

ILONA. Sped-shmed, I know better than to get myself all *distracted* by some Himbo. And whoa – I gotta run, my dad's home for dinner.

MICAH. (*holding her tightly; she tries to pull away:*) Not *yet*! *Noooo* – 'Lona – Not yeeeeet –

ILONA. (*over*) Lemme go, cutie, come on, total rarity in our house, come *on*, I can't be late. Micah –

(**JOE** *enters in a hooded sweatshirt, sunglasses.*)

JOE. Never hold a lady against her will. Hi guys, what 'you two up to?

ILONA. Gee, *I* dunno, do *you*, Mic? Maybe we both just love ducks. Well look who the peepin' perv is.

MICAH. QUACK. Why 'you watching us?

JOE. Just realized it *was* you two. I work, 'coupla blocks over, remember?

ILONA. Oh yeah? Where? Is there a school there, a tutoring academy –

JOE. Seafood place, corner of Passaic and Mountain View.

ILONA. A restaurant! Oh, so you're a chef, too! *Cool* –

JOE. No, no, a mere server, one of a coupla grunge gigs to make ends meet.

ILONA. 'Guess times are tough.

JOE. But not for Daddy. What's he into, to buy you sports cars?

ILONA. I.T. Projects Manager for some techno-crap thingy in the Citicorp.

MICAH. If I was a chef, I'd shoot one of them ducks and cook it up. QUACK.

JOE. Nice. But, up at five to catch the train? Home at nine?

MICAH. Coming early tonight, her dad. I'd make *"Duck a la Micah."* QUACK –

ILONA. Stop that. Must have news, my dad. Last time, it was to tell us he'd bought this apartment in Kipps Bay – that's this cool part of Manhattan – just for emergencies, when he works late.

JOE. But emergencies turn out to be most of the week?

(**ILONA** *glares at* **JOE**, *then turns, reaches up, seductively wipes off* **MICAH**'s *chapsticked lips. He catches one of her fingers in his mouth, playfully nibbles it. They giggle.* **JOE** *watches.*)

JOE. *(cont.)* Come by The Catch, I'll give you guys a soda or something on the house.

ILONA. Thanks, Man, but I gave up soda for Lent n' never picked up again. *Later*, Mr. Very Berry.

(**ILONA** *takes off; beat*)

JOE. You two seem tighter. You got lipstick instead of chocolate – right here. Better check when get home. Oh that's right, you hate mirrors. Micah?

(**MICAH** *wheels on* **JOE**; *an ominous threat:*)

MICAH. You gonna tell my mom? About today? About *her*?

JOE. No.

(**MICAH** *stares at* **JOE**, *then high-fives [or more up-to-date bonding gesture] him, a bit too aggressively, getting in* **JOE**'s *face:*)

MICAH. *DON'T.*

(**MICAH** *starts off, staring at* **JOE**. *Behind* **JOE**, **ANNA MARIE** *crosses in, as lights change for:*)

9.

(*Outside* **JOE**'s *restaurant; night. Shaky* **ANNA MARIE** *carries an envelope.* **JOE**'s *startled:*)

ANNA MARIE. Thought I'd scared you off. But Micah says you've kept coming. I – I'd leave your money there, but Micah'd take it. I must owe for at least three – or is it four more sessions?

JOE. 'S okay. I'm a waiter, I instinctively run a tab.

ANNA MARIE. (*handing over the envelope*) He's started to…to let you *in*. I…I don't want you to go away.

JOE. I'm still here, aren't I? You do know the "crisis" with the loquacious tatto artist isn't one. Her…kinda coming on to Micah was almost…innocent. Hard to remember how a situation like that can be…but it's not –

ANNA MARIE. (*over*) Well 'course I know it's nothing like what happened to me!

JOE. I wasn't suggesting you thought that. 'Scuse me, didn't you just ask me to stick around? Doesn't that entitle me to occasionally offer an opinion?

ANNA MARIE. (*beat; backpedaling*) Sorry. I – Somebody…*else*… snuck into Micah's bed one night – like in a movie? When a older actor starts playing a kid you got used to? One morning, this bigger version of my son walked out of his room. It'd been years since he'd…he'd hugged me, or let me – But he didn't even – Micah's hair had always smelled like this shampoo he made me buy, 'came in a bottle in the shape of "Tigger," you know, Winnie the Pooh's best fr – All of a sudden, he didn't smell anything like that anymore. Ever again. The day after – that – that girl was over – I – I could still – her perfume – I could still smell her perfume. In my house. Where she and Micah – I – I don't know how – how to

    – to – I just don't know how to do any of this!

JOE. 'S okay. Really. *Really*. I'm on the case.

(Suddenly near tears, she touches his arm. **JOE** *holds a moment, then goes. Lights up on:)*

10.

(The town library, a fall afternoon. **ILONA** *is subdued.* **MICAH** *leaps up to pace, etc.)*

MICAH. I HATE THE SMELL IN LIBRARIES. They never open WINDOWS –

ILONA. *(over)* – Shhhh, they'll kick your shapely butt outta here.

MICAH. Yours, too, so it won't be *too* bad –

ILONA. *(over)* Whisper, Babe, *whisper*. Sometimes I appreciate even the most oppressive rules. They give me something to hold onto.

MICAH. Can I ask you something else – but you can't *laugh*. Okay? Would it be, like, totally gay…if *I took* that… that "Intro to Foods" class? I walk by and I see how …how you can, like, actually learn to, like, *cook* shit, from scrat – DON'T LOOK LIKE THAT. ARE YOU *LAUGHING* AT –

ILONA. *(over)* – Shh! – Nobody's laughing at you! *Je*sus! *Gay*? Don't say that 'round my cousin János. He's a pastry chef at this French place in Berkeley, California, and a total *player*, drives a vintage Mustang –

MICAH. Cool.

ILONA. And who cares what the junior dickwads at school think of you? Their dads'll get 'em into colleges they're too dumb for, then they'll go play, like, real world Monopoly and build McMansions and ugly banks on top a' the last cow pasture in Bumblefuck, 'Jersey. Oh God, God, *God*…

MICAH. – What? WHAT 'I SAY NOW?

ILONA. It's not you, everything isn't. Suddenly, I'm having one of my "shadow days." It's not a mood that's like, *crisis*-generated. When it hits, I just get, like, sad to the 50th power.

MICAH. What 'you got to be sad about, even the *one*-th power?

ILONA. Despair, babe, despair is soooo frickin' – *pervasive*. On the way to the library, I saw this older woman, at one of those, like, one-piece stone tables nobody ever has a picnic on, 'cause, like, squirrels and chipmunks and probably rats crap all over 'em? And she was sitting on her, like, shawl or poncho thing for a cushion, all by herself, eating an *orange*. Something about the way she'd wrapped it up – so – *conscientiously* – in a hankie, covered with teensy, faded, like, violets. Old lady flowers, I can't even *think* about her. I can just picture some room she lives in – closed-tight venetian *blinds* – where she cuts up an orange and wraps it in a perfumey keepsake from her chest of drawers that's got moth balls – moth balls are so morbid – and takes it with her when she runs all her shit errands.

MICAH. Buyin' more oranges.

ILONA. If she even has enough money to.

MICAH. She could steal 'em. Nobody in a grocery'd call the cops on some starved old person, like, shoplifting *fruit*.

ILONA. But you just *sense*, she never sees another soul.

MICAH. How 'you know all that? Maybe she's gotta whole kitchen *fulla* oranges. And maybe she likes to go outside and eat in the fresh air, or if it's cloudy, maybe the orange color makes her happier. And maybe when you saw her, she was, like, just resting, on her way to meet some old dude who gave her the handkerchief, way back in, like, 1964 or something. And maybe today he'll surprise her, and kiss her wrinkly lips, and then stick his wrinkly tongue down her throat.

ILONA. Don't you dare make fun of –

MICAH. *(over)* – I'm not! The insides of her old mouth'll taste like – *hello!* – fresh *oranges!* Which *he* likes, too! And maybe that's how they *share* an orange!

(**ILONA** *breaks into a smile. With uncharacteristic tenderness,* **MICAH** *takes* **ILONA**'s *hand.*)

Just 'cause people look pathetic doesn't mean they are. There's sadder stuff – sadder *things* – than a old woman with a orange and nowhere to hang out. *Sadder.* Boy. *I* know. *Lots* sadder.

(Lights quickly come up on tense **JOE**, *in the Donato house;* **MICAH** *steps down toward him:)*

11.

(No pause; **MICAH**'s *session, in tense progress:)*

MICAH. You think I didn't haveta before?! Like in middle school? That you're the whiz-fuck who like *invented* em? That's so *lame*, "keep a journal."

JOE. This one'll be different. Not about pleasing some asshole teacher. About you. Three, four clearly stated thoughts jotted down per night. About whatever comes into your head, but *without* looking up from the page, 'hear me?

MICAH. Buncha *sentences*? No way. And don't tell me 'focus!' I don't wanna focus.

JOE. Yeah, what's up with Ilona? What goes down during those rides in her car?

MICAH. She's private. 'Not gonna talk about her. So don't fuckin' ASK.

JOE. 'Can with me.

MICAH. But I don't *haveta* if I don't *wanna*! And I don't have to tell you why.

JOE. 'Might not still know her, if it weren't for my help. Starting with the night you two met. If *I* hadn't intervened –

MICAH. – I mighta' got laid for the first time on my own living room floor!

JOE. Even better for your mom to walk in on. Haven't I been on your side?

MICAH. I got her on my side.

JOE. Listen to me! You could get into some serious shit with this –

MICAH. Y'know you're totally buggin' me tonight!

JOE. And you're bugging me!

MICAH. *(leaping into his face; shoving:)* You don't *get* to be bugged! *You* get *paid* to be here! You're a fuckin' EMPLOYEE! And can't make me write or do any shit I don't wanna do!

(MICAH turns away and JOE fully detonates, grabbing him, shoving him down on the floor or the couch. MICAH cries out, JOE pins him, using his arm, getting right in his face:)

JOE. Now you at least pretend to *get* what I'm saying. LISTEN TO ME.

(MICAH cries out, in pain; JOE tightens his grip:)

You can't focus 'cause it's always easier not to. The poor troubled fuck-up in Club Med*s* with his heavy bag of diagnoses…the reading problem the writing problem the communication problem the authority problem…the endless shit-list of reasons to be written off by everybody. Stop buying into that! You've played your L.D. card and your A.D.D. card and your O.D.D. card too damn long. Fuck your disorders – they're no excuse to dig yourself in a hole. You don't have labels tattooed on you. You gotta halfway try to just be somebody every asshole out there who's analyzed you and judged you *didn't see coming.* So stop fighting me – *STOP!* – every time I give you the best advice anybody's ever given you!

(JOE releases him. Breathless MICAH roles over, rubs his sore arm, stares at JOE; a revelation:)

MICAH. You...you were...like me.

(JOE *avoids eye contact.*)

Weren't you. When ya grabbed me, it's like you wanted to fuckin' *kill* – Shit, Man. *Whoa.* You musta been a real pisser. What all d' you do? What? TELL ME –

JOE. *(over)* ENOUGH...I did *enough*. And didn't have a pushy smart-ass around to keep me from sabotaging the few things that mattered.

(*guilty* JOE *sees him rub his injury*)

You...okay? Micah? Your arm –

MICAH. I'm cool, I'm cool.

JOE. You look – strung out. Too much Food Network? What'd ya wanna buy?

MICAH. No. No sleep...'*Caaaauuuse*, I couldn't...couldn't... *stop. You* know.

(JOE *nods knowingly.*)

Duh. Had to use, you know, like, Kleenex, so Mom wouldn't, you know, *know*.

JOE. You're not the first to figure that out.

MICAH. Do *you* – like – s*till*? Thinking 'bout who? Mom? – I don't wanna know!

JOE. And I don't wanna tell ya. Look, your chronicle – *The Strange Surprising Adventures of Micah Donato* – It'll put your scattered mind in order. No one'll see. Not even me. You can just hold it up, from 'cross the room.

MICAH. Make a deal. I'll write down shit in here, if you get Mom to let me hang out in New York.

JOE. I don't cut deals. But you've really never been?

MICAH. One time! To see these store windows ya had to wait in fuckin *line* for. "Watch out, mechanical-ized *elves*!" But after, we got to eat in, like, a hotel. 'Cause a woman Mom works with's brother is the dude 'takes ya to a table.

JOE. Maitre d'.

MICAH. And the waiter wore a tuxedo, n' gave me sparkling apple juice from France in a wine glass and kept bringing me more when I didn't even ask. And the butter – the *butter* was shaped like…like sea shells. I took a buncha boxes a' matches. Mom found 'em n' got all paranoid I was gonna start fires, but jeez – *only* good day, ever – I just wanted some fuckin' *souvenirs.*

JOE. Sea shell butters wouldn't make it back to Jersey intact. Maybe your mom would reconsider turnin' you loose in the jungle if you had the right chaperone…

MICAH. No way, 'Lona knows the city good. Lona's totally smart, too. I can, like, *talk* to her.

JOE. Who called it? Wasn't *I* the son-of-a-bitch who told ya to get to know her? Wait – one more present. Don't get excited. Just from the CVS.

(*takes out a small cheap shaving mirror*)

Sneak a peek every once in a while.

MICAH. At *myself* – no *WAY!* That's so gay –

JOE. (*over*) Micah – take a good long look. You're not so damn scary.

MICAH. (*unwilling to look; glimmer of vulnerability:*) So…so Joe…so…it gets…*all this* … gets…like…*better*, right?

(*Hit by a wave of sadness,* **JOE** *answers by giving* **MICAH** *his journal…as* **ANNA MARIE** *appears in a bathrobe. She carries a phone, dials.*)

12.

(*Late that night.* **JOE**'s *sleepless, holding a tablet of paper. His cell rings; he glances at it, illumined.*)

JOE. Hi, Anna Marie.

ANNA MARIE. Joe! I thought your voice thing'd pick up – !

JOE. (*over*) – 'S okay, I'm wide awake. Everything…*okay*? Did – Micah –

ANNA MARIE. – He's started – not just scribbling, but – *writing*. Said you asked him to. Instead of ranting in my face about ordering a spice grinder, he was holding a pen. He looked like – like he was – *thinking*. Like – a different person.

JOE. Somebody else's snuck in your house to play him now?

ANNA MARIE. Oh, Joe – his – *expression*. I just had to tell you.

JOE. Don'tcha mean thank me. You're welcome.

ANNA MARIE. Yeah, well, we'll *see*. Probably 'turn out to be a buncha chicken scratch. But it looked like *pages*. I'm probably making way too much of this –

JOE. *(over)* No you're not. How'd it happen, what'd he been up to, before?

ANNA MARIE. 'Hurt himself today – ran into a wall – or the wrong kid – so he'd been sittin' round putting ice on his arm like a patient on a doctor show. Then, flew in the bathroom for one of his new forty-minute showers. When he came out, he was just wrapped in a bedspread, maybe cause it's gotten warm again…

JOE. Indian summer night, not wasted on a fifteen-year-old.

ANNA MARIE. Then he sat down, 'hair still wet, which he usually hates – water on him.

JOE. Inspired, to express something quickly.

ANNA MARIE. I see what you're getting at. We both know he wants to write about her.

JOE. Not the girl. Himself. Whole, for a change.

ANNA MARIE. "Whole?" Micah? Come on, now, let's not go overboard –

JOE. Stop *minimizing*.

ANNA MARIE. It's just, I don't get much good news – that lasts. Another call always comes. Some kid he's elbowed ends up with a cracked rib.

JOE. 'Cause the kid called him "Sped Boy" one time too many. Look, don't read whatever he wrote. He needs to trust somebody.

ANNA MARIE. Won't be me. But he – he likes *you*, Joe. He doesn't know how to say it, but he likes you.

JOE. *(beat)* Why don't…why don't you go in…

ANNA MARIE. And do what? God, at this point, whatever you say.

JOE. Kiss him. Give him a kiss good night.

ANNA MARIE. Maybe you n' me could get another drink sometime? My treat! I've waited so long to celebrate something. Maybe just not having to handle things so alo – I gotta let you sleep. 'Night now. – Oh – Joe – Wait – I always forget to ask about your writing. 'You started anything new? I know we're not your *whole* life. *Joe?* 'Still with me?

JOE. Starting things has never been my problem. 'Night.

(**ANNA MARIE** *hangs up.* **JOE** *picks up his writing tablet. As lights fade on* **JOE**…)

(…**ANNA MARIE** *approaches* **MICAH**, *now finished writing. He shields his notebook. Exhausted, she puts up her hands, an "I'm not looking" gesture.*)

ANNA MARIE. Just don't stay up and sneak in to watch *Food*, not tonight. Is your arm okay? Let me see, what'd you go and do to yourself now –

MICAH. *Nothing.* Hey. 'Think when I'm way older – if I… when I – think I could –

ANNA MARIE. *(over)* Get another computer? We tried, you can't handle –

MICAH. *(over)* No, no, no, *no*, NO. Remember those…those little…sea shell…*butters*? At that fancy hotel that time?

(*Lost, impatient,* **ANNA MARIE** *nods wearily.*)

You think…I…could ever…be…*be…*

ANNA MARIE. "Be?" Be what – *what* – ?

MICAH. *(over)* BE…like…turn *out*…turn *into*…be…on the – for real – *real* – be…like…a chef? A chef…on the TV?

(**ANNA MARIE** *just laughs loudly. Her unintentional flash of wary cynicism stings and* **MICAH** *looks away, furious.* **ANN MARIE** *sees, and reconsidering her abruptness takes* **JOE***'s advice. She leans down to kiss* **MICAH** *goodnight.*)

(*Thrown,* **MICAH** *jerks his whole body away, putting distance between them.* **ANNA MARIE** *retreats.* **MICAH** *turns, expecting follow-up to explain his mother's unbidden show of affection. She's gone.*)

(Slamming shut the notebook, **MICAH** *stares out. Suddenly alone, he rubs his sore arm, then reaches down and pulls out the shaving mirror* **JOE** *gave him...turns it over...and very slowly raises it in front of his face. As he finally takes the smallest peek at himself, a glimmer of genuine curiosity registers...Lights fade, ending the act.)*

ACT TWO

13.

(Punk music in the dark. Lights up in the Donato backyard; early morning sun. **MICAH** *tosses back remaining chunks of sugary cereal from a variety pack-sized individual serving:)*

MICAH. Crap breakfast. 'Never let me cook. I could fix Hawaiian French toast.

ANNA MARIE. I don't have an extra half-hour to sweep up coconut.

(yanks cereal box away, determined to be upbeat)

MICAH. Wait! GIMME. I'm a growin' boy. Willya *WAIT* –

(a struggle; **ANNA MARIE** *keeps it)*

Child abuser. *CHIIIILD ABUUU* –

(wheeling as **JOE** *enters)*

– Uh-oh, what'd I do now.

ANNA MARIE. Joe!

JOE. Nothin'. Just thought I'd walk somebody to school. Do a little auditory review for that English test coming up.

ANNA MARIE. Figured you'd sleep in.

JOE. I didn't get back to sleep.

ANNA MARIE. Oh no; my fault.

JOE. Your mom called last night, hoping for voice mail; 'got the real McCoy.

MICAH. To bitch about me? What'd she say *now?*

JOE. *(a glance at* **MICAH***'s sore arm)* No complaints at the moment. You look like *you* slept okay.

ANNA MARIE. I'll say, took forever to get this one up. – Your pill. Now.

MICAH. Joe didn't have to take this shit when *he* was a kid, did ya Joe –

ANNA MARIE. Take your meds or I'm throwing out those ginger-lemon tea biscuits I found under your bed.

MICAH. Didn't steal 'em. This – friend gave me the money.

JOE. Listen – Halloween. 'Got this idea. Thought we might go in, check out the parade. In New York.

(startled **MICAH** *jerks his head over)*

'Not a school night this year. We could take the train –

ANNA MARIE. I don't like New York. It's got nothing for me.

MICAH. You hate EVERYTH – !

JOE. *(over)* – Be still. So I've gathered. So you could skip it, and I'd chaperone. And Micah? Maybe invite – what's your new friend's name again? – Ilona?

MICAH. What fun is it if you come.

JOE. A test. This boy never gets to the city, and it's only fifty minutes away –

MICAH. Thirty-eight on express trains – what kinda "parade?"

JOE. In the Village. Every freak in New York dresses up like an even weirder freak. It's way over the top. But everybody else watches, big, supportive crowd. You should see it once.

MICAH. *I'm* not dressin' up.

JOE. Nobody'd expect you to.

MICAH. Unless I could go as a "Iron Chef." Carry a great big ol cleaver.

JOE. Every instinct I have says that's a bad idea.

MICAH. Just a mask, maybe, 'one covers my whole head.

JOE. Why not, be anonymous, whole appeal of Halloween.

MICAH. Maybe 'Lona'd wanna mask, too.

JOE. Maybe; why not ask her, today –

ANNA MARIE. I DON'T LIKE BEING HIT WITH THINGS.

MICAH. 'Cause you're not open-minded, your mind's glued shut with crazy glue.

JOE. Be still. – Your mom might have sentimental feelings about Halloween.

MICAH. She don't know how to be "sentimental." Usedta be my favorite holiday.

JOE. Big surprise, an annual sugar festival.

MICAH. 'Cept candy they give out's cheap crap. She's still pissed 'cause her n' me got separated 'last time I trick r' treated. I got in deep shit.

JOE. How deep?

ANNA MARIE. The single gentleman down the street's pet was killed. Somebody lit a cherry bomb under his dog.

MICAH. *In* his dog – in his poodle's mouth or ass. And poodle, like, *parts* flew everywhere, blood n' curly fur on windshields. 'Looked like *five* poodles got blown up.

ANNA MARIE. And Micah was dressed like a – what? – a burglar –

MICAH. Ninja! *"Burglar."*

ANNA MARIE. – all in black, head to toe, I could barely see him –

MICAH. *(over)* My whole *plan*. But I *didn't* explode the dog. I liked that dog.

ANNA MARIE. During the poodle ruckus, Micah got in a fight with another boy.

MICAH. 'Kid took stuff outta my bag, like, *handfuls*.

ANNA MARIE. Micah chased him, and the boy tried to get away –

MICAH. WAIT! I just wanted my candy back. And he may have been younger, but he was way bigger n' me –

ANNA MARIE. But then Micah turned out t' be stronger, and shoved him, hard –

MICAH. *(over)* LET *ME* TELL IT. He *started* it, fuckin' *thief*. But he hit his head and got unconscious.

(**JOE** *nods, knowingly.*)

No my fault, 'asshole'd totally *stole* my trick r'treats.

ANNA MARIE. And since I'd been talking to a mother about the dog, this wave of people got between Micah and me, and the next thing I knew, he was gone.

MICAH. Poof! It was so cool...

ANNA MARIE. Like they'd just sucked him up and moved on with him –

MICAH. *(over)* – SO COOL. Coupla guys on roller blades, like, lifted me up, carried me between 'em. I fuckin' *flew.*

ANNA MARIE. The candy thief got taken off in an ambulance, but Micah was nowhere. I went door to door, then came home to call the police. He straggled in while I was on the phone, turned up the TV –

MICAH. And started boogie-*ing*! *Til!* I –

ANNA MARIE. *(over)* – vomited, all over.

MICAH. *(over)* – puked my *guts* out, all orange –

ANNA MARIE. – fluorescent orange, sprayed, like out of a paint gun –

MICAH. *(over)* WILL YA LET ME TELL IT! DID IT HAPPEN TO YOU? *NO.* IT *HAPPENED* TO ME! 'Roller bladers gave me, like, spiked Gatorade.

JOE. What about the boy who'd gotten knocked down?

MICAH. Asshole, 'turned out fine.

ANNA MARIE. But crossed the street every time he saw Micah coming. I thought his parents might sue me, but amazingly, no.

MICAH. Sue ya? For what, my "college savings?"

(**ANNA MARIE**, *exasperated, laughs ruefully.*)

JOE. You're due for a new Halloween memory. I won't let anybody drink Gatorade I haven't personally inspected. Or let the crowd suck him up.

ANNA MARIE. We'll see.

MICAH. No, I'm *going out* this Halloween –

ANNA MARIE. *(over)* I *said*, WE'LL SEE.

MICAH. *(over)* No, *no*, *NO*, I FUCKIN' *DECIDED* –

JOE. *(over)* "We'll see" works for now! Listen, 'they selling pumpkins 'round here yet?

MICAH. Hate pumpkins.

JOE. Let's jump-start the season and have ourselves a Jack o'Lantern party.

MICAH. Pumpkin pie's slimy n' makes me puke. Bobby Flay don't like it either.

JOE. We're not gonna eat it, we'll get a couple and carve faces. Drink cider, hang some Halloween decorations. And why not invite your new friend?

MICAH. Yeah, 'Lona's into art n' shit. She'd do somethin' cool –

ANNA MARIE. *N. O.*

JOE. Come on, that's the thing about these disappearing childhood holidays, you gotta reclaim 'em. I'll get all the stuff. 'Might actually be fun.

ANNA MARIE. *(beat; considering)* If we did – 'oughta just be family.

MICAH. "Family?" *He* ain't family. And don't walk me to school. That's so gay.

*(**MICAH** flies out. **JOE** gives **ANNA MARIE** a reassuring glance and runs on –)*

14.

*(– catching up to **MICAH**, moving very fast.)*

JOE. Wait up. We gotta talk. WAIT. How's your arm? Lemme see –

MICAH. It's totally no big deal. What, 'think you're, like, a fuckin' star of the WWF.

JOE. I wanna talk about you, a certain girl and what seems about to happen between you two – slow *down* –

MICAH. *(over)* Was all that, like, a set-up? Mom ask you to come over today?

JOE. Nope, my part of our bargain. Wait up, will ya? We gotta talk about what all that means.

MICAH. Told ya: private.

JOE. *Hey!* Meet me in the damn middle here. I offered to take ya to town, didn't I?

(grabs his backpack, yanks out his notebook)

Done any real writing yet in the journal?

(tug of war; **MICAH** *pulls the notebook back.)*

"Ilona." *Yeah.* Listen: You gotta be smart, gotta be cool – careful –

MICAH. I gotta go wait for her in the student parking lot –

JOE. – Listen! You *also* have to be…have to *learn* to be… *gentle.*

MICAH. "Gentle?" 'The fuck?! Get outta here, Man. 'She sees you with me, she'll take –

JOE. *(over)* MICAH, Goddamn it! If Ilona pisses ya off, you can't treat her like some little shit who stole your candy or spray-paints "sped boy" on your locker. *Okay?*

MICAH. *(absorbing this; then:)* Catch ya at tutoring. Take a extra Advil next time, maybe you can keep up.

*(***MICAH*** darts off. Lights rise on* **ANNA MARIE***, looking softer, in a new pastel outfit.)*

15.

(Outside **JOE***'s,* **ANNA MARIE** *waits; nervous. Lights change as* **JOE** *drags in, visibly in pain.)*

ANNA MARIE. You're limping. Hi. I – I just thought I'd wait. You said you usually come straight home from the –

(awkward beat; pulling out another envelope)

Oh – yeah – I – I owe you – *again* – more…

JOE. 'S okay. Thanks. Have you – ? Done something? To –

ANNA MARIE. *(over)* This *color* y' mean? Yeah, *well,* I feel like my clothes are screamin'. I wanna throw a big baggy black sweater over the whole –

JOE. Don't. 'Suits you. Nice night, let's sit out on the porch. I never do, my landlady can't complain I overuse the privilege. Look over there, near your side – autumn moonlight on Wop Puddle – wait – what was it, "*pazza?*"

ANNA MARIE. Not *pazza* – pazza means "crazy" – *pozza.*

JOE. *Pozza, "Pozza di Feoli."* You'd almost swear we were someplace else.

ANNA MARIE. If only. I always wanted to live on the water, a *sizeable* body.

JOE. Location still to be determined?

ANNA MARIE. Lambertville. On the eastern banks of the Delaware River, 'cross from this expensive town in Pennsylvania.

JOE. New Hope?

ANNA MARIE. Right, New Hope, I keep forgetting.

JOE. Your dream is the cheaper Jersey alternative? A new hope's too good for you?

ANNA MARIE. What's Joe Eskin's new hope?

JOE. On Monday, get to Wednesday. Wednesday, Friday. I tend to hope in 48 hour increments.

ANNA MARIE. What made you move here?

JOE. 'Thought you'd guessed: I grew up eleven miles west. Weymouth Ridge. Still mostly dairy farm country back then.

ANNA MARIE. Weymouth Ri – ! No! Nonna used to make us drive out there to buy tomatoes! Joe! Where'd you go to high sch –

JOE. *(a firm end to this)* Hey. Let's just say, decades later, it's still not my Lambertville.

(**JOE** *involuntarily rubs an achy knee.*)

ANNA MARIE. What's wrong with you? Joe?

JOE. I'm just a bitter sonovabitch, haven't you figur –

ANNA MARIE. *(over)* The limp, pain medicine.

JOE. *(beat)* Need 'coupla new knees, maybe a new hip… One day, everything could stop moving altogether. Won't be able to get outta bed. I have this recurring nightmare: Me, in a big ugly pothole, people stepping over me. An ER doctor told me I oughta see a Rheumatologist, "sooner rather than later."

ANNA MARIE. 'This been coming on a while?

JOE. I got old – injuries. Not exactly from extreme sports or active duty. Though war's not a bad metaphor for what brought 'em on.

ANNA MARIE. "Injuries," from – ?

(**JOE** *tenses, falls silent.*)

Somebody hurt you, Joe?

JOE. My mom…won prizes for her apple butter – spoonful of black-strap molasses, her secret ingredient…but wasn't averse to the rigors of corporal – With my dad in the VA Hospital, it was up to her to turn me into a "gentleman." If *I* shoved a kid too hard, I wasn't just denied TV privileges. I used to run – *fast*. My legs were my way – So, until I got too big for her to – She'd – She'd – I'd get – get belted to a chair. In the kitchen – Then – knees – my knees…only way *out*…were the first target…

(**JOE** *stops.* **ANNA MARIE** *reaches down, touches his knee tenderly, then takes his hand.* **JOE** *doesn't pull it away, but doesn't reciprocate.*)

ANNA MARIE. When I was a kid, I used to wake up and think the moon was shining on our *pozza*. It was always just a street lamp. Least it's the real thing tonight.

(**ANNA MARIE** *watches him a moment, then shyly leans in, gently kisses him on his cheek, and goes. More punk music blares. Lights rise on cleaned up* **MICAH**, *who walks down and stands behind –*)

16.

(*– large pumpkins on the picnic table. Charged,* **MICAH** *picks up an imposing kitchen knife and darts around the table in time to the aggressive music.* **JOE** *approaches, clicks off the boom box.*)

JOE. So you're wearing cologne now.

MICAH. Nope. New shampoo 'Lona bought me. Short Hills mall. Mom never let me have a pocket knife…

(**MICAH** *rushes up, a knife up to* **JOE**'s *throat.*)

Think I'm, like, capable of – *KILLING SOMEBODY?*

JOE. *(beat)* Put that down. Micah? NOW.

MICAH. *(threateningly, in JOE's face)* But what if I'm, like, secretly attracted to weapons?

JOE. Knock it off. 'Only knives you're attracted to are from William-Sonoma, so don't pull that with me.

MICAH. HEY, don't you make fun of me –

JOE. *(pushing the hand with the knife away)* Lighten up. Developing a sense of humor about yourself wouldn't be a bad thing to work on. But first things first: You and Ilona. Your mom's still concerned.

MICAH. That we're fucking?

(**MICAH** *just drums on the table with the knife.*)

JOE. Me, I'd assume from the aggressive knife play that you *aren't* getting any.

MICAH. Maybe it's way more n' that, 'Lona n' me.

JOE. Your mom worries you'll get hurt. I have more basic fears.

(**JOE** *slams a couple of condoms on the table.* **MICAH** *examines them, sober, serious.*)

MICAH. Not by her I won't get hurt. Everything *else*, but not 'Lona. She doesn't see me as a fuck-up. I remind her of her cool cousin who's a chef and drives a Mustang.

ILONA. *(off)* Hiiiiiii!

(**MICAH** *pockets the condoms just as* **ILONA** *arrives, popping mints. She's dressed more conservatively, wears extra make-up. She gives* **MICAH** *a warm squeeze, models a bit:*)

ILONA. Voila! Happy Hal-o-WEENIE!

MICAH. You look *different*. Like this substitute teacher we had who bragged about making her own ugly clothes.

ILONA. *(smacks him affectionately)* Watch it, Cutie. How the hell am I s'posed t' know whatcha wear to a Jack o'Lantern party.

JOE. No? Never been to one?

ILONA. We never carved out quality time for your lesser holiday festivities.

JOE. Mom didn't bake witch cookies and tape cut-out goblins to your windows?

ILONA. Mom's from Hungary, which doesn't do Halloween, and Dad's from frickin' *Rumson*, where it looks, like, low class to act too interested in a night where poor kids show up for a handout. But listen – Sir!

JOE. You seem awfully nervous about something. Tonight – ?

ILONA. No way – *but*! Sir! SIR. I have been meaning to ask you something. How many *other* students 'you got here in beautiful Mt. Morris?

JOE. Three, four; enough for pocket change –

ILONA. *(over)* Who. *Who.* Who *are* these others?

JOE. What, you want – names – ?

ILONA. – I want names. 'Cause I just noticed, all your cheapo ads got taken down. Doesn't a starving whatever like yourself need more business?

JOE. Sure, but state-certified GEPA and S.A.T. tutors are stiff competition.

(**ILONA** *flirtatiously and pointedly pulls* **MICAH***'s arms around her. A wink:*)

ILONA. Or maybe you're just a one man, one student kinda dude.

JOE. *(tense beat; then a step closer to* **ILONA***)* That's not mouthwash I smell. That's a lotta vodka and Certs.

ILONA. Back off, buddy. My parents spent the night at the New York place, I've home 'lone. I get scared. Of the dark. So I had one *teensy* taste.

JOE. Why the hell did you have any, coming here tonight?

MICAH. Don't you pick on her!

JOE. If your mom gets a whiff, she'll pick on her plenty. You can smell it all over her. Get her outta here, I'll make up an excuse.

ILONA. What's the big *whoop* –

MICAH. This is fucked!

JOE. Everything you got going for you now will be ruined. You want that?

ILONA. Hey, other kids rip off their moms' Xanax, I prefer a little *sip* of *somethin'* –

JOE. So put down that knife and get outta here!

ILONA. *(over)* – 'specially when I have to confront bullshit like this.

JOE. Anna Marie won't give a damn about your coping skills. Micah! Get her outta here before your mom comes home. *Now!*

(**ILONA** *glares at* **JOE**, *flies out,* **MICAH** *follows. Brahms's melancholy Symphony No. 3 in F/Opus 90 wafts in, as lights rise on:*)

17.

(*The car.* **ILONA**'s *head against the seat, her cell phone in her hand.* **MICAH** *reaches down to change the radio station.* **ILONA** *raps his hand.*)

ILONA. Just leave it on 'QXR! I don't wanna hear anything *superficial* that'll remind me of right now, or the last fuckin' hundred years for that matter.

MICAH. Don't get that way. Dumb Halloween shit, 'doesn't even matter.

ILONA. Something's got to matter to me! – Still no damn text message back from my parents – God, I'm so freaking predictable, the way I back myself into these *corners* – the way I… I *choose* to turn to –

(*wheels on* **MICAH**; *erratic*)

I mean, what am I doing here with – with a borderline mouthbreather. With chocolate crescents in the corners of your mouth, and…and a Ritalin eye tic… and your nails bit down to stubby little Hobbit stumps – And oh! That *guy!* – calling *me* on my – whatta con*temp*tible piece of – and *I'm*, like, standing there, fucking *participating*! God, I should be able to do so much better than all this!

MICAH. Then do better, do lots fucking better. Do it.

ILONA. Gonna smack me, 'cross the face? Huh? Ever smacked a girl? Ever want to?

(starts hitting him; lightly, but not playfully)

Ever do that? Or thatta way? Or that *hard?* HUH?

MICAH. STOP. *STOP!* I WON'T HIT YOU. I won't hit you. …I won't…hit you.

(Lights cross fade to: the living room; glasses of wine are poured; **ANNA MARIE** *drains hers:)*

ANNA MARIE. If she had a test she hadn't studied for, why'd he go, too? What, Micah's gonna help her with irregular French verbs or something?

JOE. He's smitten.

ANNA MARIE. This party was all your idea; why 'you letting him off the hook?

JOE. *(flaring slightly)* Hey. 'Just didn't work *out*, okay? She's the center of everything for him, not us. Jesus Christ he's – fifteen. *Fifteen.*

(His palpable envy hangs in the air. Music wafts in, Debussy's "Reverie." Lights rise on **ILONA***'s car,* **ILONA***'s head resting in* **MICAH***'s lap:)*

ILONA. Wish I was eight again. On vacation in the Adirondaks. In a pool with water that's too cold. And my dad bundles me up in a towel that smells like bleach, and we all shiver and stretch out in big wooden chairs that hurt if your ass is too bony, so Dad puts me in his lap, and my fingers pucker up and turn white and Dad blows on 'em to warm me up.

MICAH. Rich people's trip.

ILONA. I got an earache and we had to leave this restaurant Dad made reservations in three months in advance, right in the middle of dinner. But there were five days when everybody didn't have a fist in their stomachs.

MICAH. I'd like to bundle ya up in a towel. 'N blow on your fingertips. I'd like to do lotsa things – I'd like to…to… bake you a birthday cake.

ILONA. Ohmigo – that's so incredibly sweet – and I'm such a turbo-bitch to you –

(**MICAH** *leans in to kiss her.*)

We can't. I – smell – like –

MICAH. *(blows in his hand; sniffs)* So? Me, too. Hazelnut. Truffles.

ILONA. What *is* a "truff –

(**MICAH** *kisses her again, gaining confidence.*)

MICAH. 'Smell like ya did the night ya tattooed me. You were drunk then.

ILONA. *(takes out vodka bottle)* Maybe it's time you n' me just got lit together, totally slammed –

MICAH. Pour it out. DO IT. You do that, I'll stop taking my shit.

(**MICAH** *pulls her close as lights shift.* **ANNA MARIE***'s loosened from the wine, too giddily invested in the romantic atmosphere to notice* **JOE***'s reserve. "Reverie" continues softly under:*)

ANNA MARIE. Oh Joe, I'm sorry. I am. I trust you. You're always so sensible about him.

JOE. The coolly detached commentary's my specialty. Easy, from the sidelines.

ANNA MARIE. *(inadvertently touching his hand)* But are you, by now? Just on the sidelines? 'Not where Micah wants you. Or I want you.

JOE. Right; all you need's a damn cripple on your back.

ANNA MARIE. *(laughs, pouring wine in both glasses)* "Too?" *Salute! A cent' anni!*

JOE. *(clicking glass in toast) Salute.* Cent anni, what the hell is that, 'hundred years?

ANNA MARIE. I know, a stretch for a guy who only looks ahead two days! Joe Joe Joe Joe *Joe*. I'm okay, Joe, *okay* for once! As long as we – *I!* – got you – here! Hey! – how come no woman ever caught you.

JOE. What makes you so damn sure I was worth catching.

ANNA MARIE. Aw come on, you? *You – ?!*

JOE. *(over)* – I can get claustrophobic, too. 'Maybe not enough make me throw iceballs at people. 'Least not lately.

ANNA MARIE. Well ya coulda fooled me! Do you know *I* haven't done *this*…in *cent' anni*? *Since* – God – waaaay before…But you won't believe it, but I've thought about – the…the *possibility* – almost since you started with Micah. Since – that stormy day! By the pond! – when I told you I might come let ya wait on me at the Sea Catch? In *fact*…I…have – fantasies, now. Fantasies. 'First time in so long.

(silence; **JOE** *tenses, avoids eye contact)*

JOE. Musta' been before you found out about my ol' crumbly knees.

ANNA MARIE. Your knees are just fine.

(touches his leg; blushes, but has to get it out now)

Some late night when…when I don't have a mustard stain on my blouse…and the deodorant I've had on since five o'clock in the morning. Micah's in his room, out. And I'm in a nightgown – 'first time since I was twelve and pretended t' be Wendy in *Peter Pan* – and I…I see…the moon. Moonlight, moon *beams* on the pond through my window. Moonbeams on you, Joe. You sneak in. We don't even talk. Micah doesn't hear… doesn't even wake up…

*(***ANNA MARIE*** startles* **JOE** *– and herself – and kisses him. To be chivalric,* **JOE** *responds slightly. They pull back, hold a minute.* **ANNA MARIE** *looks down. Not knowing how to extricate himself,* **JOE** *touches her hand – an ambiguous gesture to halt the romance which might be construed as a promise of more. He stands, slowly goes.* **ANNA MARIE** *watches, visibly stirred.)*

(As lights fade on **ANNA MARIE**, *they rise on* **MICAH**, *alone, ready to burst, holding a phone.)*

18.

(Lights up on **JOE**, *answering, disoriented:)*

MICAH. 'S me.

JOE. Hey.

MICAH. *'Happened!*

JOE. What hap – Ilona?

MICAH. I fucked her. We fucked each – *"we made loooove."* I – *You* know, right away. Then we waited, n' listened to her radio, like, old time-y piano music – *classical* – 'Lona's into all that, too! Then we – you know, *again*, and I didn't – not so fast –

JOE. Back up –

MICAH. – Don't tell me I shouldn't. I'm gonna do it with her whenever I want to.

JOE. Hang on, don't talk so loud, you'll wake your mom.

MICAH. She's, like, out, 'cause *you* two had wine. She wasn't even pissed when I came home. Kept saying "Joe's a good man..." What'd you do to her tonight? Get her lit?

JOE. So – all this was equally cool with Ilona? And you used a rubb – ?

MICAH. 'Course it was cool – I'm gonna make love to her whenever I want. Nobody can make me stop. So don't go getting all, like, Doc Eskin on me –

JOE. *(over)* Did you use the condoms I –

MICAH. Yeah, yeah, she takes meds or some shit anyways. – DON'T TALK ABOUT IT. Ruins it. *Totally.* I gotta fuckin' crash now, Man.

JOE. I know I said to, but I wouldn't put this in your journal. *Micah?*

MICAH. I'm not writing any lame journal anymore. I don't know where it even is. I don't wanna do nothin' else now. Just wanna be with her.

*(***MICAH** *clicks off, as lights dim on* **JOE**. **MICAH** *glances in the shaving mirror again, studies his reflection, as if looking for some latest change in himself. Lights rise again on* **ILONA**, *nervously walking along the pond embankment:)*

19.

(JOE *arrives at the pond.* ILONA*'s on alert.*)

ILONA. Make this fast, I gotta huge test tomorrow in World Civ.

JOE. What is that, some kinda A.P. course – ?

ILONA. What, what, what, Man, *what,* wanna talk *academics?* You don't have a right to demand covert meetings.

JOE. I'm not worried about your grades. The vodka. An everyday thing?

(ILONA *starts to bolt.* JOE *unzips her backpack.*)

ILONA. HEEEYYY, Buddy! You got no fuckin' *right* – !

(a struggle; he extracts an Absolut miniature)

Oh get over it! A few *shots.* I know Merit Finalists headin' to Princeton with 24/7 weed habits. So let's just say, "It's something I'm working on."

JOE. How, by drinking more? Nobody else has caught on?

ILONA. You can't threaten me. Go on, tell Mic's mom. I'll get over it. I'll get over Mic. He's a cute boy, but *just* a cute boy.

JOE. By now, he's gotta be more than that to you.

ILONA. And to you, too, Mister.

(Her cell rings. Lights up on MICAH, *at home.)*

Shit – Hiiii there cutie, whassup?

MICAH. Wanna hang out, take another *drive* out by Chimney Rock? Listen to some more tunes on 'QXR – ?

ILONA. Not the best time, Babe, gotta call ya ba –

MICAH. *(over)* Wait! So second period, right, I get sent to my counselor. And I'm all, like, "What 'I done now." And he goes, "Asked to take that class, *remember?"* Cool, huh. *Hey?* You better call later. Promise? *Promi* – ?

ILONA. *(over)* 'Promise-promise-promise, now go learn how to make Baked Alaska n' tell me 'bout it later.

(ILONA *hangs up; lights fade on* MICAH.)

ILONA. *(cont.)* He is precious, the little chef-in-training. But very temporary. And that means, if you take some big, like, stepdaddy action to break us up, I will not go *off* myself.

JOE. You think *I* want to stop you guys from seeing each other?

ILONA. Who cares, I don't sit up at night, trying to figure you out —

JOE. *Hey,* time out. Truce. With amnesty? Come on, what the hell 'you doing to yourself, swilling this crap to get through the day?

ILONA. What the fuck do you know about my day? Who asked you to be *my* counselor? Just 'cause my dad doesn't make it home for pizza night doesn't mean I wanna play mind games with some *case*. What's in it for you, anyway? I usedta wonder if you were just queer for Micah.

JOE. And that's why I encouraged his being friends with you?

ILONA. 'Matchmaking shit could just be a big cover. To keep people from wondering if you secretly go for not-so-little boys?

(taunting, up in his face)

Keep 'em from wondering why a poor...totally clueless —

JOE. Stop that.

ILONA. — *pussy* like you —

JOE. Knock it off —

ILONA. Gets off on "tutoring" a horny teenager you practically *adopted.*

(a step back, realizing:)

And *what's* with all the *prep* today? Look at you: Showered n' shaved. Hair combed. Even put on an ironed shirt for a change. All to hang out and play Rehab with *me*? All of a sudden you, like, clean up like a player? Anna Marie never gets all *this*.

JOE. Nothing 'bout me has a damn thing to do with your vodka prob –

ILONA. *(new appraisal)* WAIT, wait, wait, wait, *wait*. I never figured you actually wanted to fuck me yourself… but…*but* … it's not like you *don't* want to, either. Huh? What's wrong, Anna Marie not puttin' out?

(**JOE** *just stares.*)

Or maybe it wouldn't matter if she did. Maybe…*she* never got the big Joe Eskin *makeover*…'cause you don't give a shit about getting in *her* pants.

(quiet revelation)

Shit, Man! That *day*…right *here*…watching Mic and me make out. You *are* a perv, aren't ya?

JOE. Don't call me –

ILONA. *(over)* – All this time, coaching Mic in way more than English. Shit, the lame pumpkin party…setting up little, like, "excursions" for us *three*…even buying his damn rubbers…

JOE. All 'cause I'm Micah's friend. Apparently, his only real –

ILONA. – who wants detailed reports on how good he gets laid.

JOE. But if it's all so temporary and you don't care about him, then you're playing with fire.

ILONA. Like *you're* not. And his mom's totally clueless, isn't she? Clueless…that what you really want…isn't *her*…but…to *watch*…us.

JOE. *(beat)* You're a bright girl. With a real vicious streak. And a real problem with alcohol.

ILONA. And when you try to play cool, it's all show. Nothing cool's going on. You're, like, wasted. Boy, wouldn't ol' Anna Marie love to know about *this* little rendezvous with her kid's girlfriend. Don't worry, Mister Joe. I'll make the lady feel better. Let her know she's not missing out. I mean, even with too much cheap cologne to cover the fried fish stink, you're still the same loser underneath.

(**JOE** *grabs her purse, goes for her phone.*)

JOE. Go on, call. 'Course I should probably make a call myself. Bet ya Daddy'd haul-ass back from the city real quick if he knew you're getting shit-faced every day to screw a Sped in that car he bought you.

ILONA. Like you have the balls to call. And if you did, like my father would believe some…some – *diner* waiter. Or even *take* a call from a loser like you. "Player?" Perv. *Total* pervert –

JOE. *I told you, don't call me that.*

(**JOE** *lunges for her, grabbing her arm.*)

ILONA. Let the fuck go of me, Man. LET ME THE FUCK GOOO –

(**ILONA** *pulls free, and slips, falling on the ground. Enraged* **JOE** *darts toward her, but then instantly stops himself, and takes a step back.*)

(**ILONA** *cowers.* **JOE** *collects himself, then leaves.* **ILONA** *grabs her purse, takes out her vodka and sits on the bench. As lights dim on* **ILONA**, **ANNA MARIE** *and* **MICAH** *appear in their living room.*)

20.

(**MICAH** *hands* **ANNA MARIE** *a paper. She breaks into a smile, throws her arms around him. Phone rings. Lights rise again on* **ILONA**, *dialing them:*)

ANNA MARIE. Hello?

ILONA. It's Ilona – Lawlor, Ms. Donato –

ANNA MARIE. Oh, hello! How are you, Hon!

ILONA. *(over)* I'm good, I'm good. Sorry, I kinda need to talk to Mic.

ANNA MARIE. Oh, sure, sure. Ilona –

MICAH. That's 'Lona! Gimme –

ANNA MARIE. – while I have you on the phone, I want to, I guess, apologize. For –

MICAH. GIMME THE PHONE.

ANNA MARIE. *(over)* – seeming – I don't know – unfriendly sometimes.

ILONA. 'Case ya haven't noticed, I'm not easily insulted. And I'm sorry I missed the, uh, you know, uh, pumpkin cutting thingy.

ANNA MARIE. Oh no, Micah and Joe tell me you're in some pretty tough honors classes. We'll all get together another time –

MICAH. *(grabs the phone;* **ANNA MARIE** *retreats)* Where ya been, it's been hours!

ILONA. What happened to Mommy, 'she been taken over by a pod person?

MICAH. She's, like, high I got a B on a test. Minus. Woulda been a D if they counted spelling. But still.

ILONA. I'd say but still. Well, how cool's that. Maybe it's time to go it *alone.*

MICAH. Alone how? You don't wanna –

ILONA. Not me, Dumb-Dumb. *Cutie.* Time to dump Mr. Joe.

MICAH. But Joe's the one 'helped me get the B min –

ILONA. *(over)* So now you don't need him. Get Mom to cut him loose. She can do whatever she wants, date him, have another kid with him. You don't haveta buy in.

MICAH. But wait, wait – hold it – what's Joe done?

ILONA. He's always just *there.* I don't like him, I'm sorry, I tried, but, he creeped me out from the start. And then – today –

*(***ILONA*** winces at her own slip-up.)*

MICAH. Today? Today *what?*

ILONA. Nothing, I just figured out Joe's gotta go. Look, I'll tutor in English, too.

MICAH. But Friday – remember? – New York.

ILONA. *That,* ick. 'Supposed to rain. Buncha, like, amped boys prancin' in wet girl clothes, whoop-de-fuckin' *do.*

MICAH. But it's the first time Mom'll let me. She's totally psyched cause a' Joe.

ILONA. Then let's you and me break *away* from him. I'll figure out how.

MICAH. But it could fuck up the whole thing, and she'll never let me go agai –

ILONA. Will you please not *whine* about it? Leave it to me to figure out a way to make it "accidental." Oh Babe, I'm way smarter n' Eskin.

MICAH. I hate to, like, pull somethin' on Joe. He's –

ILONA. Say "my friend" and you're never taking a long ride in my car again.

MICAH. Joe's not a asshole.

ILONA. What if he is? What if he's, like, irrevocably fucked up?

MICAH. You having one of your *days*?

ILONA. Listen, I gotta go try to pull a B minus, too. Don't worry about how we lose Jumpin' Joe. I'm totally on the case.

(She hangs up, takes a pull on her Absolut miniature. **MICAH** *dials. Lights rise on* **JOE***:)*

MICAH. 'S me. Got that test back. Got a B. *Minus.*

JOE. That's incred – a *B* – that's just – your *mom* – she must be on the ceil –

MICAH. *(over, erratic)* You like 'Lona, right? Right?

JOE. Is your mom worried about her again? Micah, f*ocus.* Did she find out? Did you write about it in your journal?

MICAH. 'Told ya I'm not doing no journal. Anyways, Lona and Mom are getting along good.

JOE. Has Ilona said something to you –

MICAH. *(over, erratic)* This sounds way fucked, but – but you – you like *me*, too, don't ya?

JOE. Do I *like* you?

MICAH. You're…you're my Crusoe, I'm fuckin' Friday. Right? *Right?*

JOE. Or the reverse. Sometimes, I almost think of us as the same person.

MICAH. Like "before and after." Me, before, you – you whenever.

(**ILONA** *unscrews the top of the bottle. Elsewhere,* **ANNA MARIE** *appears in a robe, brushing her hair. She drops her hand to gently caress herself. Stops.* **JOE** *picks up* Robinson Crusoe, *opens it.* **ILONA** *sniffs the vodka, recaps it.* **MICAH** *picks up his journal, flips it open, tosses it aside. Lights dim, as sounds of a subway waft in:*)

21.

(*New York City. Lights up on the interior of a subway car.* **MICAH** *has a scary mask around his neck.* **ILONA** *is plugged into her iPod. The car stalled,* **MICAH** *leaps up, claustrophobic.*)

MICAH. Why 'we stopped so long?

ILONA. Halloween, every fruitcake's heading downtown, the freak Mecca.

JOE. You heard the announcement; we'll move soon.

MICAH. 'S hot in here.

JOE. No it's not; you just think it is. Sit down.

MICAH. Maybe it's, like, a bomb.

ILONA. Babe, it's not a bomb, just too many asshole people.

MICAH. *(to offstage riders:)* WHAT ARE YOU STARIN' AT?

JOE. Jesus, Micah, will you just sit!

ILONA. *(coded, to* **MICAH***)* When we *get* there, *things* get better. *Remember?* Trust me: 'Next *stop*.

JOE. It's actually two, the next is 14th, we get off at Christopher, Sheridan Square. Did you stop taking your meds? Last few days?

MICAH. 'While back.

ILONA. It's his body.

JOE. Sit down.

MICAH. I don't wanna, I'm thirsty and gotta pee.

ILONA. Hold it, babe; you can do it 'tween parked cars in a few. My dad does it.

JOE. *(takes out a notebook)* Here – write something. If you don't wanna write, draw a picture.

ILONA. He's not in frickin' pre-school.

JOE. Micah? – come play Hangman with me –

ILONA. If standing's better than Sesame Street 2.0 with you, what's it to ya?

MICAH. *(shoving JOE away)* No fuckin' air in here.

JOE. Sit down, count backwards from twenty.

MICAH. 'S worse, I wanna open a window –

JOE. Don't touch the windows.

MICAH. Why the fuck are we stopped so *long*?!

JOE. SIT DOWN.

ILONA. HE DOESN'T HAVETA. Nobody asked for your opinion. You're not his shrink, Pervert.

MICAH. *(jerks his hand away, pulls out a knife)* Stop yellin'!

JOE. What the hell 'you doin' with that?

MICAH. Parta' my costume.

JOE. Well put it away, or I'm taking it. NOW. You wanna get arrested?

ILONA. Better listen to Pervert.

JOE. We're moving again.

(**MICAH** *wheels around, stares at* **JOE**, *shoves the knife in his pants.* **ILONA** *throws the notebook at* **JOE**. *Lights shift to reveal:*)

22.

(A subway platform at 14th Street. All three are lined up. **JOE** *keeps a nervous eye on* **MICAH**.*)*

JOE. Don't get any closer than the bumpy orange line.

ILONA. He's not gonna *jump* –

JOE. *(over)* Micah, god*damn* it, don't lean out like that!

(**MICAH** *nervously teeters, peering into the tunnel.*)

Let's go, we can walk the rest of the way.

ILONA. I don't wanna walk in the rain, we oughta just head back.

MICAH. I wanna see the parade, I wanna see *something*.

ILONA. Let's vote. Mic, wouldn't Penn Station be lots better? Dry, bathrooms? Pizza? And those hot cinnamon pretzels you like?

JOE. After we see a piece of the parade.

ILONA. The way-gay menagerie? What's in all that freak shit for you, Perv?

JOE. One quick flash of something *else*. Besides Mt. Morris. Micah? Besides the inside of your house. Inside of your *mind*. An escape. Like you did once. Your mom told me you took off in the snowstorm.

MICAH. I was fuckin' brave when I was a kid.

JOE. Be brave again, don't let anybody stop you.

ILONA. Oooh, "wisdom." How'd ya even get the night off? Star waiter like you? Did you go and get yourself fired, Perv?

MICAH. Why 'you keep callin' him that?

JOE. Let's get on the next train. Here. Just do this.

(*He tries to give the notebook to* **MICAH**. **MICAH** *grabs his hand, shoves it away.*)

MICAH. Tell me why you call him that! TELL ME!

ILONA. 'Cause he finally proved – a pervert's what he is. *All* he is.

(**MICAH** *wheels around on* **JOE**; *he takes a step closer, betrayed, silently demanding answers:*)

ILONA. *(cont.)* Tell him. TELL HIM. How ya just had to meet me.

MICAH. *Meet* her? 'The fuck?

JOE. Outdoors. My side of the pond. Broad daylight. Only 'cause she'd turned up drunk for your party.

MICAH. Why didn't ya tell me you went?

ILONA. Why 'ya think? I was right next to him when you called – about seeing your guidance counselor, remember? He was totally pimped. – Weren't you?! Cologne. New shirt from the sale-table at the Gap. Like a big whoop-de-do hook-up. – Admit it, Man! A halfwit woulda seen you wanted in my pants!

MICAH. You…you hit on her?

JOE. I did not and she knows it. I was trying to make things better for you both with your mom.

ILONA. Yeah, by meeting me, all showered n' shaved, without tellin' *him?*

JOE. Micah, she's got a problem –

ILONA. Yeah, YOU. Tell him how you did yourself up to meet me!

JOE. – She's sneaking vodka tonight, too – smell her breath. She gets you to stop taking your meds cold fuckin' turkey, but she's always boozing –

ILONA. It's Halloween, Pervert, I will party in the festive manner I choose.

(**MICAH** *pulls away; betrayed, cut to the quick:*)

MICAH. WAIT. Why didn't you ask me to come with you? Why'd you go talk to her and not even tell me?

ILONA. He just had to get close to what *you* have, to the ass you're getting.

MICAH. *No way! Ilona?* Joe? *Joe?!* What – what about my *mom?!*

ILONA. See, that's the sick deal, Babe, he could give a crap about Mommy. The freak's *watching* us and gets ya to write about fucking me, 'cause it turns him on.

(**MICAH** *reaches down, pulls out the knife.*)

MICAH. Stop screaming!

ILONA. Mic – Babe – put that away.

JOE. Just give that to me, Micah.

(*sound of train*)

MICAH. Stop telling me what to do! You – you were supposed to *not* be an asshole.

JOE. So I'm an asshole. Don't you be one, slow down and think for once. *Think*. And give me that knife.

ILONA. Drop it, Babe, we can go get ya a sugar coated pretzel and forget this shit. I mean it. Let's lose him, like we planned on! Let's lose him for good!

(train sounds; it grows closer)

JOE. Damn it, you're acting like a loser, a five-year-*old* los –

MICAH. DON'T YOU CALL ME THAT. NOT – *YOU*.

*(**MICAH** darts at **JOE** pulls his arm behind him, holds out the knife; ear-splitting subway noise as the train roars into the station, lights flashing. An impulse passes through **MICAH**.)*

JOE. Hey – hey – sorry – *sorry* –

*(But once the train clears them, **MICAH** overrides his impulse; shuddering, he just shoves **JOE** out of his way, safely to the inside of the platform; he drops the knife out of sight. **JOE** stumbles to the side.)*

JOE. Micah…Micah…you gotta know by now…I care about you.

*(**JOE** reaches out for him, looking in his eyes. **JOE** throws his arms around him, hugs him tightly.)*

It's all so you don't end up like me.

*(Beat, then **ILONA** laughs cynically, jarring **MICAH**. Startled and humiliated, **MICAH** shoves **JOE** down on the platform. Freaked **ILONA** tugs on **MICAH** to flee. **MICAH** holds, stares down at **JOE**, frozen. Stumbling to his feet, **JOE** picks up **MICAH**'s notebook, holds it out:)*

JOE. Micah?

*(**MICAH** looks back one last time and then exits with **ILONA**. Lights dim. A harsh, tinny subway horn blares off-pitch through a tunnel. Lights rise on:)*

23.

(A corner near Penn Station. **MICAH** *races in,* **ILONA** *following him.)*

ILONA. Hey trick or *treat*, Babe! Couldja maybe just *speak* to me a sec?!

*(***ILONA** *catches up, breathless.)*

Okay, *be* pissed, but I handled it, didn't I? 'Finally got the prick to leave us alone. Je-*sus*, *he's* the loser – !

MICAH. *(over)* – I – I – *Almost* – but I…didn't –

ILONA. *(over)* – Didn't what, *what?*

MICAH. I…I was gonna – *gonna* – to Joe – back there – when…when the…the *train* – but I *didn't*.

ILONA. Shit – what time is it? – Tomorrow my Dad's finally driving me to see his college, gonna show me 'round his campus. I've gotta be – gotta prove – gotta be – be on top of my *game*. Sharp!

MICAH. "Focused."

ILONA. *(whipping out NJ Transit schedule)* Damn straight. Oh great, the ten-thirty-eight's 'bout to pull out, and here we are. Come on, babe, let's run, we can still make it! Come *on* – !

MICAH. *(over)* – No. You go.

ILONA. What?! Come on – !

MICAH. I'll get home on my own.

ILONA. Right, gonna jump on a train all by yourself, "Here's my ticket, Mister Conductor Man!"

MICAH. I can take care of MYSELF.

ILONA. I know ya can, Babe, I was joking. I *was*. I'm sorry. Maybe I shoulda told you about Joe when it happened – it wasn't to be mean or keep a secret. I was thinking of you. Honest.

MICAH. 'Cause…it don't mean shit what we do…you still think I'm the same dumbfuck you stuck the tattoo on. You're just gonna drop me off for good whatever day *you* decide to. ADMIT IT.

ILONA. *(deflated; a sad revelation:)* But y'know what? If only… if *only* you n' me had been in the same damn grade. Bet we woulda' hung out on the playground together and taken on everybody…Totally helped each other just fuckin' cope. Oh *hell* yeah. Micah? Micah? Still gonna bake me a birthday cake? Maybe I should bake you one.

MICAH. Just go. *Now.* Didn't ya hear me, GO.

(**MICAH** *shoves her away. She starts to cry, and for a second refuses to move. But finally runs off. Lights fade, and rise on* **ANNA MARIE**, *pale, exhausted. As she takes a step down:*)

24.

(The Donato living room. **MICAH** *enters; he sits with his back to his mother.)*

ANNA MARIE. Third time she's called. If you don't want to talk to her, tell her.

MICAH. She'll get it. 'Said what I gotta say to her.

ANNA MARIE. I made an appointment with a new doctor over in Montclair. "Upper," aren't *we* finally moving up in the – Can't see you till 4:30 on the sixth. That means not 'til this Thursd –

MICAH. *(over)* I read calendars. I know November sixth is Thursday.

ANNA MARIE. Had some thick accent, I had to keep apologizing after every word, saying I couldn't understand her. I'm so sick of apologizing. I told her you'd stopped your meds too sudden, we need to get back on track. She asked if you'd ever been diagnosed as bi-polar, and if we'd tried Strattera. It's not a stimulant and can take a while to kick in –

MICAH. *(over)* – I'm not in Club Meds anymore.

ANNA MARIE. Good for you, but we both know exactly when things started to go ba –

MICAH. *(over)* Didn't you hear me, I just *said* I'm not taking drugs anymore.

(**ANNA MARIE** *picks up a small cardboard box, pulls a form out:*)

ANNA MARIE. Great, but you're flunking again. Gotta email at work from your English teacher, you haven't turned in assignments in two weeks. And I found some schedule change, for January. What, some kinda Home Ec class to replace study hall? You need study hall. Here. You left it next to my bed. "The Everyday Gourmet," it says. That's you all right –

(**MICAH** *snatches the paper from her hand.*)

MICAH. It's "Introduction to *Food*" and it's important. To *me*. I put it there so you'd sign it. So do it. SIGN IT.

ANNA MARIE. *(doing so, shaken; then looking down in the box)* I…I got a call from this nasty landlady 'cross the pond. Eleven o'clock on a Sunday night… 'Seems our friend took off without paying his November rent.

*(startled **MICAH** glances up at her)*

And did *I* have any *idea* where he mighta' got to? She found our number in the crap he left behind. Probably on a matchbook. So now I'm the…the "next of kin" to some dud who gets around in boxcars.

MICAH. *(this registers)* Joe took off.

ANNA MARIE. Joe. Joe isn't even "Joe." When I said Eskin, she says his checks say Jody Mack Clarey. Our Man of Mystery used an alias. *Used*…a lot….

(emotion overtakes her; a painful, abrupt turn)

We kissed each other. Once. I wanted to kiss him more. Every time I saw him. Planned on it –

(**MICAH** *turns away;* **ANNA MARIE** *pulls a notebook from the box:*)

The landlady went through Joe's room. Didn't find

any spare change, but Joe did leave his masterpiece behind. A story – big shock – Joe'd only started. Looks juicy, all seven n' a half pages of it.

(**MICAH**'s *head jerks up; he moves closer to take a look.* **ANNA MARIE** *opens the notebook, scans pages, stops at the end. She begins to read aloud:*)

ANNA MARIE. "...And then it was clearer...as if a blindfold had been ripped from my eyes...as if a mask without eyeholes had been taken off...we...we were one and the same...

(**MICAH** *takes it from her hands, looks at it.*)

Joe's story just stops. Like Joe.

(**ANNA MARIE** *moves closer, puts a shaky hand out, then, with a graceful resolution, touches* **MICAH**'s *face. Their foreheads momentarily touch; a rare, very tender connection, she looks in his eyes. The phone rings.* **ANNA MARIE** *exits, leaving* **MICAH** *alone, looking down at* **JOE**'s *book. The ringing stops. He reads aloud:*)

MICAH. "...we were one and the same...He and I...Where I...I left...left off...Friday. Friday – *Friday* –

(*he cries out; involuntarily:*)

FRIDAY.

(**MICAH**'s *suddenly hit with an unprecedented and overpowering sense of loss.*)

Friday...seemed to begin; where I was long finished, he was just beginning."

(**MICAH** *pulls himself together, then, with* **JOE**'s *notebook in hand, carefully smoothes out the class form* **ANNA MARIE** *signed and sticks it in the back. He reaches down, fumbles in* **JOE**'s *box until he produces a pencil stub. He shakily turns the page, then puts the pencil to the page.*)

(**MICAH** *holds, then slowly, tentatively, begins writing on the page where* **JOE** *left off. And* **MICAH** *again continues to write...now very pointedly not looking up from the page...as lights fade, ending the play.*)

COSTUME PLOT

ACT ONE
1.
MICAH
Distressed/stained cargo shorts
Ripped, dirty, chocolate-stained tee-shirt
No shoes

JOE
Khaki slacks
Denim shirt
Weathered leather lace-up work boots
Vintage worn leather belt

ANNA MARIE
Brown cotton Capri pants
Loose faded floral print blouse
Sandals
Shoulder bag

2.
MICAH
Distressed cotton shorts
Wrinkled short-sleeved shirt
Distressed sneakers; no socks

JOE
Same khakis and work boots
Change to: colored cotton tee-shirt

3.
ANNA MARIE
Loose, patterned or faux-Madras summer dress
Unstructured cotton jacket
Same sandals, same bag

JOE
Same khakis/tee-shirt; add: aged denim jean jacket
Same work boots

MICAH
Same shorts, remove shirt (i.e. shirtless under apron)
Add: large distressed and stained white chef's apron
No shoes

4.
MICAH
Same shorts; remove apron, add: wrinkled buttoned shirt
Sneakers, no socks

JOE
Same khakis, tee-shirt, work boots; add: tan/brown summer
Sports jacket

ANNA MARIE
Same dress, minus jacket; add: pastel cotton cardigan
Same shoes, same shoulder bag

5.
MICAH, JOE, ANNA MARIE
Same

ILONA
Denim designer short-shorts
Tank top
Casual, opened designer blouse
Designer heels, belt
Designer purse

6.
MICAH
Same; add: applied tattoo to bare chest

JOE, ANNA MARIE, ILONA
Same

7.
JOE
Same, minus sports jacket

MICAH
Same shorts; change to: knit pullover shirt
Same sneakers, no socks

8.
MICAH
Same, add: nylon windbreaker

JOE
Same, add "hoodie" hooded sweatshirt, sunglasses

ILONA
New designer jeans
Casual designer blouse
New sneakers

9.
JOE
Same, minus sunglasses

ANNA MARIE
Jeans
Loose cotton v-neck sweater over tee-shirt
Casual slip-on shoes

10.
MICAH
Distressed torn jeans (i.e. knees ripped out, etc.)
Distressed tee-shirt
Outgrown/ill-fitting thin cotton jacket
Sneakers, no socks

ILONA
Same designer jeans; change to: tank top
Add casual cotton cardigan
Same sneakers

11.
JOE
Faded Levi's ("501's" or equiv.)
Dark tee-shirt
Denim shirt (scene 1) open
Same work boots

MICAH
Same

12.
JOE
Same, minus denim shirt, minus shoes/socks

ANNA MARIE
Faded pastel terrycloth bathrobe
Slippers

MICAH
Same, minus: jacket, shirt, shoes (i.e. shirtless, jeans only)
Wet/damp hair

ACT TWO
13.
JOE
Same faded Levi's and work boots
Plaid or striped long-sleeved shirt buttoned over dark tee-shirt

ANNA MARIE
Denim skirt
Long sleeved autumn blouse
Low leather pumps

MICAH
Same jeans
Change to: bright tee-shirt
Open/out wrinkled shirt

14.
Same

15.
ANNA MARIE
New tailored, two-piece pastel ensemble
New low-heeled sandals or pumps
Same shoulder bag

JOE
Same Levi's; shirt now opened over dark tee-shirt

16.
JOE
Remove (over) shirt, add sports jacket over dark tee-shirt

MICAH
Same ripped jeans
White long underwear shirt
Black tee-shirt with rock band insignia and graphics

ILONA
Peasant-styled skirt
Matching blouse
Elegant silk scarf
New heels
New shoulder bag

17.
ILONA, MICAH
Same

ANNA MARIE
New semi-dressy tan skirt
New elegant black silk blouse
Simple gold necklace
New hairstyle

JOE
Same

18.
JOE
Same, minus sports jacket

MICAH
Same jeans, same white long underwear shirt minus tee-shirt minus shoes

19.
JOE
Same Levi's; change to long-sleeved, fitted black designer shirt (out)
New chic, dark, running shoes
Hair combed/re-styled

ILONA
Pleated Burberry/plaid miniskirt
Tailored blouse
Sweater
High-heeled soft leather boots
Shoulder bag

20.
ANNA MARIE
Old jeans
Cotton v-necked sweater
Change to: terrycloth robe

MICAH
Same jeans, same white long underwear shirt; add: colored tee-Shirt
Same sneakers

ILONA, JOE
Same as scene 19

21. - 23.
JOE
Same Levi's; change to: red tee-shirt
Denim jean jacket (scene 3)
Black Halloween eye mask (around neck)
Same new running shoes

MICAH
Same jeans, long underwear shirt; add: dark, zippered neckline sweatshirt
Classic monster/devil Halloween mask
Belt with makeshift holster for knife

ILONA
Designer jeans
Tank top
Chic autumn jacket
Pastel/white Halloween eye mask (around neck)
Same sneakers

24.
ANNA MARIE
Brown Capri pants (scene 1)
Unstructured cotton jacket (scene 3)

MICAH
Same jeans
Change to dark long underwear shirt

PROPERTIES PLOT

ACT ONE

1.
Older model boom box
Opened box of imported gourmet cookies
Extra/loose (softened, melting) chocolate-frosted cookies
Distressed/taped-together Game Boy or equivalent
Worn brown leather satchel (**JOE**)
New small spiral notebook
Small bottle of generic ibuprofen with substitute (candy) pills

2.
Distressed backpack (**MICAH**)
Worn brown leather satchel (scene 1, **JOE**)
Duplicate spiral notebook (scene 1) with scribbled/doodled pages
paperback edition, Robinson Crusoe

3.
Makeshift paper fan
Older model cell phone (**ANNA MARIE**)
Home phone (land-line; wireless receiver)
Chipped mixing bowl
Distressed wooden spoon

4.
Toenail clipper
Bright pink 4x6 index card with handwriting
Duplicate (scene 1) distressed spiral notebook
Duplicate (scene 2) distressed paperback Robinson Crusoe
Backpack (scene 2, **MICAH**)

5.
2 beer bottles half filled with substitute liquid
Twenty-five dollars (cash)
Absolut vodka miniature filled with water

6.
Water-soluble tattoo
Boom box (scene 1)
Grocery bag with (unseen) ice cream cartons inside

7.
Duplicate (scene 1) distressed spiral notebook with more entries
Duplicate (scene 2) more distressed paperback Robinson Crusoe

8.
Girl's pastel backpack (**ILONA**)

9.
Sealed #10 envelope with {unseen} bills inside

10.
Library book(s)
Girl's pastel backpack (scene 8, **ILONA**)

11.
Worn brown leather satchel (scene 1, **JOE**)
Pocket-sized shaving mirror
Marble cover-styled composition book/journal

12.
Home phone (scene 3)
Cell phone (**JOE**)
Paper tablet
Pencil
Duplicate (scene 11) marble cover-styled composition book, with entries
Pen

ACT TWO

13.
Individual boxed serving of cereal (from "variety pack")
Milk
Spoon
Pill (candy) on saucer/dish

14.
Backpack (scene 2, **MICAH**)
Marble cover-styled composition book (scene 11)

15.
Sealed #10 envelope with {unseen} bills inside (reused, scene 9.)

16.
Boom box (scene 1)
2 uncarved pumpkins
Large kitchen knife
2 foil packages of condoms
Certs/breath mints

17.
Wine bottle with substitute liquid
2 wine glasses, half-filled with substitute liquid
Absolut vodka miniature filled with water
iPhone (i.e. state-of-the-art cell) (**ILONA**)

18.
Cell phone (scene 12., **JOE**)
Duplicate (or reused, scene 11) small shaving mirror

19.
Girl's pastel backpack (scene 8, **ILONA**)
Absolut vodka miniature filled with water
iPhone (scene 17, **ILONA**)
home phone (scene 3)

20.
English test (answers inked in, graded)
Duplicate (scene 11) marble cover-styled composition book with entries
Home phone (scene 3)
iPhone (scene 17, **ILONA**)
Cell phone (scene 12, **JOE**)
Hair brush
Distressed paperback Robinson Crusoe (scene 7 version)
Absolut vodka miniature filled with water

21.- 22.
iPod with ear buds
New small spiral notebook
Kitchen knife

23.
Wrinkled NJ Transit train schedule

24.
Distressed cardboard carton
Loose papers (torn from tablet in scene 12)
High school guidance department form with hand-written entries
New marble cover-styled composition book with handwritten entries
Pen
Pencil stub

THE SETTING

ODD is best served by a simple unit set, allowing instantaneous and fluid transitions between scenes. Full blackouts should occur only at the end of each act. In the initial production at Premiere Stages, director John Wooten and designer Joseph Gourley placed the audience on two sides and created a vivid wooden game board-like structure. Scenes were staged on planked walkways lining the perimeter of the playing area, a series of higher platforms, and for the Donato backyard, the center floor. Since this is a story about attempts to contain or defuse aggression, narrow, restrictive platforms allow key confrontations to be played in seemingly claustrophobic spaces. But elevations are not required. A level proscenium stage will work equally well, with changes in lighting employed to differentiate locales. All furnishings should be minimal and if possible stationary throughout the action. The only literal pieces needed are a distressed picnic table and bench for the yard, and an aging couch and easy chair for the Donato living room. Everything else — the bar, library, pond banks, porch and the NYC subway and car — can be suggested with a few movable stools and inverted cubes.

From the Reviews of
ODD...

"The transformation of the fringe player to someone possibly acceptable by mainstream or even upper-class society, the man who breezes into town and energizes the young man with a disability, the man with troubles of his own who solves a family's troubles: These are classic human stories and *ODD* melds them well while bringing them to 2007...

ODD asks who is broken — the people whose disorders are gaping, bleeding wounds, or the people weighed down by their life challenges...

The winner of Premiere Stages' Play Festival, *ODD* is an important work at a time when befuddled parents want to fix their kids with a pill: better living through chemistry."

- Gannett/Home News Tribune

**Also by
Hal Corley...**

Easter Monday

Mama and Jack Carew

Please visit our website **samuelfrench.com** for complete descriptions and licensing information.

www.ingramcontent.com/pod-product-compliance
Lightning Source LLC
Chambersburg PA
CBHW070647300426
44111CB00013B/2302